Sue Arnold

Sue Arnold was born in India after her mother had escaped from the Japanese advance on Burma, and the family came to live in England at the end of the war. After a degree in English at Trinity College, Dublin, she did stints on the *Tehran Journal*, the *Blackburn Evening Telegraph* and the London *Evening Standard* before going to work for the *Observer* where she has been a regular and highly popular columnist. Winner of the Magazine Writer of the Year Award in 1983 (after being runner up the year before), her columns were collected for publication, as *Curiouser and Curiouser*, in 1985. She has also written *Little Princes* (1981) and is a regular contributor to magazines including *Radio Times*, *Homes and Gardens*, *Good Housekeeping* and *Cosmopolitan*. She is married with six children.

D0530474

SCEPTRE

Also by Sue Arnold

Little Princes
Curiouser and Curiouser

A
Burmese
Legacy

SUE ARNOLD

SCEPTRE

First published in 1995 by Hodder and Stoughton
First published in paperback in 1996 by Hodder and Stoughton
A division of Hodder Headline PLC
A Sceptre Paperback

10 9 8 7 6 5 4 3 2 1

British Library Cataloguing in Publication Data

Arnold, Sue
  Burmese Legacy
  I. Title
  959.1040922

  ISBN 0 340 66005 8

Typeset by Palimpsest Book Production Limited,
Polmont, Stirlingshire
Printed and bound in Great Britain by
Cox and Wyman Ltd, Reading, Berkshire

Hodder and Stoughton
A division of Hodder Headline PLC
338 Euston Road
London NW1 3BH

To my mother
without whom – not a lot

Contents

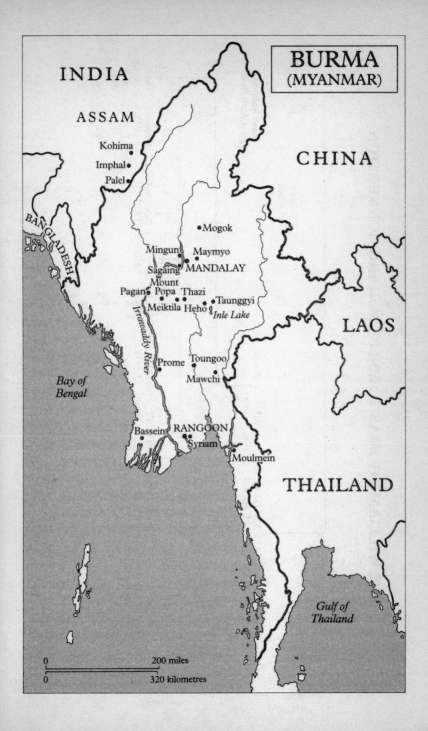

BURMA
(MYANMAR)

INDIA

ASSAM

CHINA

BANGLADESH

Kohima

Imphal

Palel

Mogok

Mingun   Maymyo

Sagaing   MANDALAY

Mount

Pagan   Popa   Thazi

Meiktila Heho   Taunggyi

Inle Lake

Irrawaddy River

LAOS

Bay of
Bengal

Prome   Toungoo

Mawchi

Bassein   RANGOON

Syriam

Moulmein

THAILAND

Gulf of
Thailand

0   200 miles

0   320 kilometres

THE WILLIAM THOMAS TOWNLEY McHARG CONNECTION

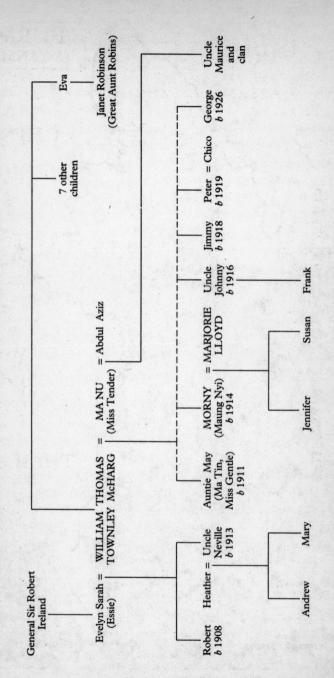

THE CHARLIE LLOYD CONNECTION

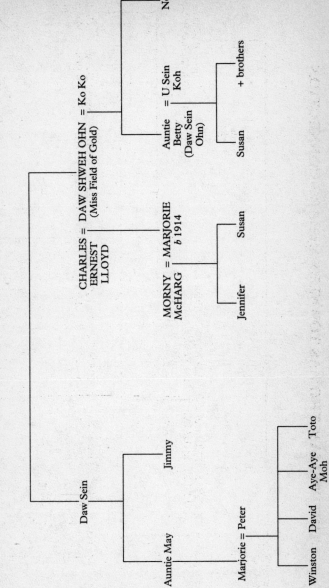

Feeling English

All I ever wanted was to be English. I feel English. I think English. I sound as plummily English as the girl who answers the telephone in the Fine Art department of Sotheby's thanks to a succession of well-heeled private schools in the Home Counties from three of which I was expelled but that's another story. The trouble is I don't look English and for all the soul-mateyness I know I share with the woman in tweeds ordering double damask table napkins at the General Trading Company in Sloane Street I know from long experience that were she and I to fall into conversation, sooner rather than later she would ask 'Where are you from?'

'Chelsea,' I reply. Well it works sometimes. Her eyelids flicker in confusion; she rummages uncertainly in her handbag aware that I am stalling but too polite to pursue the subject. The English are so polite.

When the *Observer* moved offices from Blackfriars to Battersea five years ago, Princess Alexandra was invited to preside over the official opening. Members of the editorial staff gathered in the boardroom to be received. It was an afternoon in midsummer and extremely hot. The boardroom had floor-to-ceiling plate-glass windows, the Princess was late and we were beginning to stew. 'Gosh, it's warm,' I remarked to Mrs Robinson next to me. She was married to someone on the board. Mrs Robinson looked at me curiously. 'Yes, isn't it,' she agreed, 'though I dare say you're used to the heat where you come from.' It is perfectly in order, however, to be both polite and curious in England.

'No, I mean where are you from originally?' persists my new friend at the General Trading Company linen counter, and there's no escape.

Now here's the strange bit. I don't know why I do it but I always have and probably always will. I preamble. It's that word 'originally'. It has sinister anthropological overtones. It conjures up pictures of caves and wall paintings of people with low foreheads and long arms. 'Burma,' I should rap out brightly and then order my own set of double damask napery. But I don't. 'It's all a bit complicated,' I begin. 'You see I have two British grandfathers, one Welsh, one Scottish, from the Borders I believe (my maiden name is McHarg), and two Burmese grandmothers which means that both my parents are half so I suppose that makes me half Burmese too.'

My interlocutor stretches her eyes and cries, with the same surprised rapture as Women's Institute coach parties from Macclesfield when the curtains open on the set of *Miss Saigon*, 'Oh, how exotic.' She will then tell me all about a delightful little person she knew who came from Japan or Jaipur or Jakarta because to the English, all Orientals are the same.

Not being pure Burmese, merely sallow-skinned and dark-haired, I could come from almost anywhere south of the Simplon and east of Suez. During my year as a student in the United States I slotted comfortably into whatever ethnic minority happened to be around – Puerto Rican in New York, Navaho in Niagara, Mexican in Texas, Chinese in San Francisco. Someone in Vancouver thought I was Eskimo. But no, I am half Burmese and the fact that until relatively recently I have neither known nor wanted to know anything about my origins (that word again) stems principally from the fact that I was ashamed of them. It wasn't my fault. It was my mother's. And to be fair it wasn't her fault either. It was society's – isn't it always – and it was conditioning.

When we arrived in England on a troop-ship from Rangoon after the war, my mother, my older sister and me aged three, a colour bar was openly practised in Britain. 'No Blacks' said the signs in the boarding-house windows where my mother was enquiring about accommodation. 'And no coloureds either,' said the landlady when she saw us.

'But we aren't coloured,' my mother insisted. 'The Burmese are of the brown races like the Siamese and Malays. Africans are black, Indians are coloured but the Burmese are a brown race.'

She is a self-confessed racist. Everything Enoch Powell said she agreed with whole-heartedly, especially his desire to repatriate immigrants. 'Quite right too,' said my mother, nodding at the television screen and Mr Powell's jabbing finger.

'But Mum, don't you understand? You'd be on the first boat back to Rangoon.'

'Nonsense, Susan, the Burmese are different. They are gentle and pose no threat like all these Africans and Jamaicans and Indians.'

Of all the immigrant groups it is the Indians for whom my mother reserves a special contempt. This, I am led to believe, is less a personal than a national characteristic. The Burmese look down on their Indian neighbours who were brought in as cheap labour. They call them not just *Kalas*, meaning

Indians, but *kway Kalas* meaning dog-Indians. And it was obvious from the start that the English in England looked down on the dog-Burmese. The only way to cope was to pretend ignorance. I didn't ask about my roots because I didn't want to know about them. Why should I? Looking foreign was a bore. More than a bore, an actual pain. The pain of having the other children in the class call me Blackie, when I disliked black people as much as my mother did.

I came across an old photograph of myself the other day in one of my parents' ornately padded photograph albums. It showed me aged around seven in my Convent of St Francis de Sales school uniform. I was no beauty – small, stocky, awkward, with a big moon face, flat nose, cropped hair and round wire National Health glasses, the kind that much, much later, John Lennon was to make fashionable, but which in the 'fifties were regarded as pathetic. My mother, who had a Confucian-style adage to suit every occasion, said that as far as their children were concerned, the English were like dogs, whereas the Burmese were like swans.

'English children are cuddly and pink with big eyes and floppy limbs, all very winsome and endearing, like puppies,' my mother would explain, 'but just see how ugly they grow up. The Burmese are exactly the opposite. Burmese children are like stiff, awkward little cygnets, nothing much to look at when they're young, but then look how beautiful they become.'

I'm not sure that my telling the boys who tried to sting my bare knees with nettles after school that their mothers were dogs while mine was a swan would have done me much good. I used to run weeping with terror out of the school gates (this was Mount Stuart in Kenton, North London, the state school I went to in between the posh privates), and desperately attach myself to the nearest passing grown-up. 'Please, please can I walk home with you?' I would beg. I was a paedophile's dream. Just as well I was so unappealing.

My way of defending myself was to be top of the class. They would respect my intellect, I reasoned, and forget my sallow skin. I was not only top of the class at Mount Stuart but two years ahead of my peer group, my elevation being due principally to my ability to do joined-up writing. I'd learned how at the Convent. Far from making the boys with the nettles who called me Blackie respect me, it made them – as I should have realised had I been less clever and more intelligent – hate me more and bully me harder.

The woman at the General Trading Company has just finished telling me about every oriental connection she has ever had, including her son-in-law's Filipino nanny. 'It must be wonderful to have such exotic roots,' she sighs. Must it? I'd rather come from Chipping Norton and look pale and horsy and English like her. I wasn't even born in Burma, or Myanmar as it is now officially known. I was born in India and only spent a few months in Burma as a baby before we came to England. 'I suppose it is rather exotic,' I say and from my dismissive tone it is clear that I have no further wish to discuss my origins.

Who knows how long this lack of interest might have lasted had the editor not called me into his office one morning in the summer of 1985 and said he wanted me to cover the Royal Tour of China in September. The press would assemble in Hong Kong, then fly in specially chartered planes accompanying Her Majesty for a week. I mentioned this assignment to a close friend with whom I occasionally make my more adventurous expeditions. Gaye had always wanted to visit Burma and I had always resisted. But now, with China beckoning, Gaye raised the subject once more.

'Listen, Sue,' she coaxed, 'Hong Kong is practically next door to Rangoon. Take a week off, we'll meet in Bangkok, get our visas and go. I know you have a hang-up about your relations. Stuff your relations. I want to see the pagodas in Pagan. Mind you,' she added, 'if I had a ready-made network of relatives out there, I'd use them. If nothing else we would save on hotel bills.'

Stay with my Burmese relations? Was she mad? How could we? They were primitive, spoke no English, wore *longyis*, ate with their fingers and lived in – I tried hard to picture where these mysterious relatives of mine might live. In mud huts? No, that was Africa. In jungle clearings perhaps. My mother was always talking about the jungle. Both her first and second husbands had worked there in the teak business. Technically, I'm sure they were called forests but my mother has always been prone to colourful exaggeration. When she achieved the ambition of a lifetime by marrying a white man (her description) and moving to our house in Hampshire, surrounded by rhododendrons, she referred to this too as jungle and spent months hacking feverishly at it with billhook and axe. 'We've got to keep the jungle down,' she would explain to neighbours who came for tea.

And then I remembered a story she once told me about her own mother during the war. My grandmother had fled Taunggyi when the Japanese occupied the town, taking her younger daughter (my Auntie Betty) with her, and went to live in a stilt house on the Inle Lake. Tourists to Burma will know the Inle Lake which is famous for its leg-rowers.

'Every night,' this is my mother talking, 'Mummy would wrap her jewels which represented all the wealth she possessed in a cloth pouch and tie it to the end of a long rope let through a small hole she had made in the floor under her mattress, and she would go to sleep holding the end of the rope, the other attached to the jewel pouch dangling in the water, in case the Japanese came.'

'And did they?' I asked.

'Yes,' said my mother. 'One day they arrived on the Inle Lake and told my grandmother that she was under arrest.' Her late husband, Ko Ko, my mother's stepfather, who had been a successful broker in Taunggyi, had embezzled funds belonging to the government, they claimed, and converted them into jewels for his wife. They had orders to confiscate the jewels and take my grandmother back to Taunggyi for trial. My grandmother knew it was hopeless to pretend. You don't mess with a detachment of Japanese soldiers. We all know that. In Britain especially we are accustomed to horrific stories of Japanese war crimes but my grandmother's experience is relatively tame. They could easily have bayoneted the defenceless old woman and then helped themselves to her jewels but they didn't. They were reasonable.

It was the same later when they came to her house in Taunggyi saying they knew she had a young girl living with her, my Auntie Betty. My grandmother denied it, although Betty was hiding upstairs, and the Japanese soldiers believed her and went away. They were looking for Burmese girls to be nurses in the newly established field hospitals which were filling up with wounded Japanese. Auntie Betty played the Anne Frank game throughout the Japanese occupation and just as well she did if you believe another of my mother's wartime stories. When the British finally won Burma back on the tennis court at Kohima the Japanese shot all the Burmese nurses as they retreated rather, they said, than have them nurse white men.

But the Japanese asking my grandmother for her jewels in her stilt house on the Inle Lake were polite. 'Where are the jewels?' they said and my tiny, frightened grandmother lifted up the mattress and pulled up the rope with her precious package on the end. She then got into the boat with the soldiers and they started to row to the shore.

We have some pictures at home made of black and gold

straw sent one Christmas by relatives in Taunggyi. They show silhouettes of stilt houses on a lake surrounded by palm trees and a big yellow moon in the middle. When my mother told me the story of the Jewels on the Rope I thought of the pictures and mentally added another silhouette – a long rowing boat, full of soldiers and guns and a small, stooped figure with her hair drawn back in a bun. My grandmother always wore her hair in a bun with a circle of fresh jasmine round it. Half-way across the lake they passed another boat occupied by the Saw Bwa, the Burmese equivalent of an Indian princeling. He came from the neighbouring district of Ming Shweh but knew my grandmother well.

'Why Auntie,' said the Saw Bwa, 'what are you doing? Where are these soldiers taking you?'

'They are taking me for trial in Taunggyi,' said my grandmother. 'They say Ko Ko stole the money to buy my jewels and they have taken them away from me.'

In vain the Saw Bwa protested her innocence. He did however manage to persuade the soldiers to row my grandmother over to his residence on the far side of the lake where every piece of her jewellery was itemised in a ledger so that when they were returned to her, as he knew they would be, she could check that there was nothing missing. The story had a happy ending. 'Auntie, what are you doing here?' said the judge, dismissing the case out of hand.

'By the way,' said my mother at the end of this saga, 'do you know who the Saw Bwa was?'

'No,' I said.

'You know that picture next to the fireplace at North Lodge?' (North Lodge was our house in Hampshire.) 'Well, he was the father.'

I thought about the pictures at North Lodge. My mother favoured Boots for art works. There was a portrait of a chubby little lad with tousled hair, rosebud mouth and quivering lower lip, one blue saucer eye blurred where a small puddle has formed on the lower lash. The picture was entitled 'Toby in Tears'. My mother had hung it in the hall. 'It's amazing how a really good artist can capture a mood,' she would say to visitors, pausing as they hung up their coats. Surely the Saw Bwa of Ming Shweh couldn't be the father of Toby in Tears.

'No, of course he wasn't, Susan. I mean the picture of Saw Ohn Nyun.'

In its day it was as popular and as ubiquitous as Trechikov's Green-faced Lady. It shows a beautiful, serene Burmese maiden kneeling demurely in a cream silk *longyi*, her upswept hair coiled in glossy Nefertiti profusion and studded with jewelled combs. She is a Shan princess and her father was the Saw Bwa of Ming Shweh, the man who helped my grandmother. I know the story is true but I still wanted to laugh. It was like someone telling you that the Laughing Cavalier's father had helped your grandmother apply for her bus pass.

Now, talking to Gaye about a visit to the pagodas of Pagan, I was also imagining us travelling to the Inle Lake and spending a few days in a fragile house above the water on stilts surrounded by lilies. It sounded interesting.

'I suppose I could find out who we might stay with in Burma,' I conceded.

Now here's a curious thing. Up till now I have been talking exclusively about my mother's attitude to being Burmese, her perception of England, her prejudices and hang-ups, but it turned out to be my father who dropped the bombshell about my antecedents.

My parents divorced when I was seven. My mother was granted custody of the children and until recently I hardly knew my father. I forget the precise circumstances of the revelation. I must have been asking him which of his many relatives we might stay with. He had far more than my mother, three brothers, three half-brothers, a sister and endless cousins, aunts, nephews and nieces all over the country. My father, unlike my mother, is steady, placid and not given to exaggeration. He has an unusual name, Morny McHarg. I used to think Morny was a variation of that old-fashioned soap-maker Mornay, a favourite with Burmese ladies, along with Pond's Cold Cream, Max Factor and Tangee lipstick. Either that or a diminutive of Mornington, just the sort of silly pompous Christian name the Anglo-Burmese would relish. In fact it is neither. It is the nearest you can get in English to the Burmese Maung-nyi – *Maung* meaning boy and *nyi* meaning red, from the reddish tinge to his hair. My father got so fed up explaining to people at his North London tennis club that Morny didn't stand for Mornington that in the end he said, 'Just call me Mac.'

'Tell me about my grandfather,' I asked him. 'How did he meet your mother? When did they get married?'

'They never got married,' said my father placidly. 'It wasn't like that in Burma. They didn't have marriage ceremonies like you have in England. But anyway, even if they had, my father couldn't have married my mother. He already had a wife at home in England.'

Pow. There it was, slap in the middle of my respectable English drawing-room with the William Morris wallpaper and freshly plumped-up cushions and the invitation on the mantelpiece. We were bastards. Burmese bastards. At one of my posh boarding-schools a girl called Gillian Armitage told the housemistress she refused to sleep next to Alix Saunders in Blue dorm because, she claimed, Alix was illegitimate. How she came by the information no one knew. Not many of us knew what illegitimate meant, but it sounded disgraceful. This was the po-faced 'fifties. They hadn't invented love children yet and only Shakespeare went in for bastards.

'Are you really illegitimate?' I had asked Alix with interest, as if it were a medical condition, just as now, thirty years later, I was asking my father, with what must have sounded like vintage Mary Whitehouse severity, 'Does that mean we're illegitimate?'

'I suppose so,' he said. 'It was different in those days.'

And that's how it all started. Suddenly I wanted to find out about 'those days'. I wanted to know about the two British grandfathers and the two Burmese grandmothers, the quartet that up till now I had dismissed with disinterest, embarrassment and shame. All I ever wanted was to be English and now I found I had a ready-made English family to hand. The quest had started.

The English Connection

My grandfather, William Thomas Townley McHarg, had eight children, two legitimate English ones and six Burmese bastards. His only daughter, my Auntie May born 1911, was the oldest of the Burmese brood. My father Morny, born three years later, was his oldest Burmese son. His birth date, 4 March 1914, is significant. My grandfather's contribution to the Great War effort (at forty-nine he was too old for active service) was to move his Burmese mistress into his government bungalow, and produce three more sons – Johnny in 1916, Jimmy 1918 and Peter 1919. A fifth child, George, born while my grandfather was on home leave in 1926, died in infancy. When in 1926 my grandfather retired from the ICS (same initials different name: it was now the Indian Civil Service since the word Imperial had fallen out of favour), he left Burma for ever and went home to England. His wife, Evelyn Sarah, and their two sons Robert, born 1908, and Neville, born 1913, were waiting for him.

It couldn't have been much of a home-coming. You can see by the birth dates of his first four children that William

Thomas Townley was a bit of a bastard himself. Syncopated infidelity you might call it – one white child, one brown, one white, one brown – a variation on a rhythm method.

My father laughs proudly and says that William Thomas Townley was a randy old devil, but then my father was on the winning side because my grandfather openly favoured what his wife's family referred to as 'the coloured relations'. Would everything, I wonder, have been different if his first son Robert had not been a cripple? It was because of Robert's handicap that my English step-grandmother, Evelyn Sarah Ireland, had brought him home to England. Burma at the turn of the century was not a comfortable place for colonial wives. It had none of the Memsahib tradition that India, with its centuries of colonial experience, enjoyed. Burma was raw, difficult, unsociable and for Evelyn Sarah, or Essie as she was known, with a sickly baby in tow, it was impossible. So Essie went home to her mother and the comforts of the family house in Southsea, opposite the Isle of Wight. William stayed on to work his way up the ICS ladder.

How long after Essie's ship sailed into the sunset he met my grandmother, Ma Nu, I don't know, not more that a year if the dates are anything to go by, because in the spring of 1911 my Auntie May was born. Whether news of this, the first of 'the coloured relations', reached Southsea is another mystery. Probably not. William was by now working up-country in Prome. Communications were primitive. On the other hand Essie's younger sister, Dolly, may still have been in Rangoon and heard rumours. It was because of Dolly that Essie Ireland had come to Burma in the first place. Dolly was engaged to a Lieutenant Ames who was serving with the British Army in Rangoon. Essie, the oldest of five Ireland sisters, had come out as Dolly's chaperone.

The Ireland sisters must still have been together in

England in 1893, because that was the year another sister, Amy, was married. It was by all accounts a very grand wedding in Derby. Her sisters Evelyn Sarah, Nancy, Sybil and Dolly were maids of honour and each received a silver brooch with the date 1893 fashioned in pearls in the middle. There was also a brother, Gordon, known as Jock. Details of Amy's wedding and a list of her wedding presents were reported in *The Times*. Her gifts included six fur coats, three shot-guns and three revolvers – not the usual line in Victorian wedding presents but the couple were emigrating to the Northern Territories of Canada, a great deal more dangerous and a lot colder than Burma.

So Essie and Dolly take ship, arriving in Rangoon in 1902, and in the months leading up to Dolly's wedding Essie meets my grandfather at the races. They fall in love, she cancels her passage home and in 1906 they are married. He was forty-one, she was ten years younger. Their wedding photograph shows a handsome couple, he standing stiff and straight, hand on hip in stylised music-hall pose, she sitting on a wicker chair with orchids in her veil and more in her bouquet. She looks sweet and gentle and pretty, leaning a little towards him. The most striking features about my grandfather are his high forehead, which I have inherited, and his unfriendly staring eyes which I hope I haven't.

My Auntie May's Burmese name is Ma Tin, Miss Gentle. She may well have been a gentle baby. William Thomas Townley, the randy old devil, didn't stick around long enough to find out. I think of him as William Thomas Townley because my father refers to him this way, pronouncing each name slowly and proudly like a role of honour. My father's half-brother, Neville Townley McHarg, was the result of the first home leave my grandfather took as a married man. He may have been a gentle child too. He was certainly very small, but again William Thomas Townley didn't exactly linger to see his second son into the world. He was back on the high seas heading East. Eleven months later, with a two-month sea passage in between, my father was born in the District Forest Officer's residence in Prome.

I wonder whether Essie sent pictures of *her* new baby out to Burma. I hope she didn't. From what I can gather, William Thomas Townley liked strapping, tough, healthy people around him. Neville was none of these. He was frail, slight and always small for his age. The main reason my grandfather objected to the idea of Neville going to Dartmouth rather than Haileybury, apart from the cost (Dartmouth was £100 more expensive), was that he thought Neville would be too small to go into the Navy. This was in 1926 when my grandfather had retired from the ICS and come home to be head of his English family. Neville, thirteen by now, had set his heart on going to Dartmouth. Father and son clashed violently over the issue. Essie backed Neville, less I would have thought to please her son than to displease her husband for whom she bore a deep and unforgiving resentment verging in later years on hatred. Mother and son got their way, but it was a struggle. Neville went to Dartmouth, didn't exactly shoot up, but achieved enough inches to become an officer. He ended up a commander.

Fifty years later Essie would have divorced her husband and started again, but Edwardian ladies weren't like that. She gritted her teeth, shut her eyes and thought of William's salary. The Irelands were not wealthy, her father was a colonel in the British Army when she married, and District Forest Officers in the Imperial Civil Service were well paid. It was when William insisted on sending money to the coloured relations long after he retired that the real bitterness set in. My grandfather paid for all his children, English and Burmese, to go to private school and university. Neville, at home from Dartmouth for the holidays, remembers his mother's anxiety about money. Poor Essie. She must have led a dog's life. An unfaithful husband is a hard row to hoe, even though the row he was hoeing was ten thousand miles away. It should have been out of sight out of mind but the steady stream of letters arriving from Burma for her husband (the children all wrote regularly) and the one written in return never allowed Essie to forget.

The more I think about her wretched situation, the handicapped son, the unfaithful husband, the lonely existence in Southsea, the more sympathy I have for her. I know she's nothing to do with me, her life impinging on mine only by the finest spider's-web thread, but I do somehow feel an affinity. Maybe it's second-generation guilt. And then I have to stop and ask myself some leading questions. I put it to you, Susan Hilary Marjorie McHarg, that you only conceived this touching sympathy for your step-grandmother when you discovered that she had grand English connections. I put it to you that had this Essie, who sounds more like an obsolete domestic heating appliance than an English lady, been the daughter of a coal merchant, or even a bank manager, you wouldn't be quite so generous with your solicitude. Finally, I put it to you Mrs Susan Hilary Hutchison née McHarg, thence Arnold divorced, that your self-confessed ambition to be English, to be Ms WASP, with the emphasis on the White, has so befuddled your brains that you seriously expect us to believe you give a fig for the finer feelings of the wife of your lecherous, concupiscent and downright blackguardly grandfather. I rest my case.

Was it really only when I discovered that my step-grandmother's parents were General Sir Robert and Lady Ireland that I gave poor Essie's situation a second thought? And how did I find out about her grand connections anyway? Through Uncle Neville, of course. It was Great-Aunt Robins who told me about the brave commander. She was my grandfather's niece, the daughter of his youngest sister

Eva. William was the oldest of nine McHarg children, Eva the youngest. Great-Aunt Robins never married. Her real name was Janet Robinson but we called her Great-Aunt Robins from the start. In Burma you always address women as Auntie, not only small children but adults too out of respect. The middle-aged Burmese doctor in Brighton with four grown-up children still calls my mother Auntie. Great-Aunt Robins was my grandfather's confidante, the only person in England to whom he talked about his Burmese family. I met her not long after we arrived in England. We had come from Windermere where we had been staying for a few days with my grandfather and Essie, and William Thomas Townley must have urged his daughter-in-law, my mother, to take his granddaughters over to see her. He probably wanted to know what she made of us. She lived in Teddington at 33 Langham Road, the same sturdy semi-detached villa in which she died at eighty-seven.

I don't remember much about those early visits, although they became regular monthly excursions until Jenny and I went to boarding-school. Then they dwindled to maybe once or twice a year until, when my parents divorced, they stopped altogether. I vaguely remember a dark, oppressive house with lots of fussy ornaments and lace mats which we were told not to touch. There was a big Victoria-plum tree in the garden which Jenny and I were sent out to climb while my mother and Great-Aunt Robins talked over the teacups.

It's funny how silly things jog your memory. Twenty years later, when I was a cub reporter working for 'Londoner's Diary' on the *Evening Standard*, I was sent to interview the veteran actor Richard Goolden who was playing Mole for the umpteenth time in the annual West End production of *Wind in the Willows*. Mr Goolden lived in a pretty little house in Oakley Street, Chelsea, the nearest thing to a mole hole you can imagine. It was so cluttered with furniture and books and pictures stacked against the walls and theatre programmes in untidy lop-sided piles, you had to burrow your way into the back room. The actor was sitting behind a beautifully laid tea table. He poured Earl Grey, then offered a plate of biscuits, chocolate fingers and those rectangular pink wafers the colour of dentures, meticulously arranged in the shape of a wheel and a chocolate marshmallow in the middle.

'Good heavens,' I said, 'do you know that is exactly how my Great-Aunt Robins used to arrange the biscuits when we went to tea in Teddington.'

In 1948 Great-Aunt Robins couldn't have been more than forty-five, twelve years older than my mother, but to me she seemed ancient. What would she be like now, I wondered, as my mother and I drove out to Teddington three decades later on the trail of the English connection? Walking down Langham Road with its respectable houses, neat front gardens and swathed net curtains, I tried to see it all as my mother would first have seen it forty years earlier with her naïve immigrant's eyes. Did she hold 33 Langham Road as the touchstone against which our new houses in London should be measured? We were living in rented accommodation in the Bayswater Road, my mother having presumably persuaded the landlady that the Burmese were not coloured but of the brown races. But we were looking for our own house.

I'm not sure how we ended up in Kenton. It may have been because my mother had got herself a job as a secretary in Perivale or that may have come after we bought the house. She doesn't remember.

'I just know that I saw this house for sale, 34 Christchurch Avenue. It cost £800 and I bought it with cash.'

Thirty-four Christchurch Avenue was not as classy a semi as 33 Langham Road but it had aspirations, and it was an improvement on our last rented address, a downstairs flat in Kenton Road with a couple of nudists upstairs. I remember that very well. The woman was called Rita and she came down to collect the newspaper every morning wearing only fluffy slippers. Christchurch Avenue, the estate agent told my mother, was a socially desirable street because of its superior architecture. All the houses had bay windows. Thirty-four Christchurch was a cut above its neighbours because it had proper curved bay windows, not square ones. Square bays were better than no bays at all, but everyone agreed that curved bays were best. There was a half-way stage. There were houses that had curved bays on the ground floor and ordinary flat windows above, but we had both and we felt very proud.

It must have been after a few teas at Langham Road that my mother cottoned on to another nicety of suburban mores. Unlike Christchurch Avenue where, apart from the windows, the houses were identical red-brick boxes, the houses in Langham Road were different. Some had gables with Tudor beams, some had little crenellated overhangs, some had front doors set back in porches with mullioned windows, some had their front doors daringly at the side. A street with the courage to contain variety was definitely an upwardly mobile street and a couple of years after buying 34 Christchurch we moved onwards and upwards to 126 Woodcock Hill, Kenton, where not only was every pair of semis glamorously different from its neighbour but, most desirable of all, it had detached houses too. To live in a detached house on Woodcock Hill was to have arrived. They stood aloof, alone and coveted.

It was only when my mother ran away with my stepfather and they bought a tiny two-bedroomed hunting lodge in a Hampshire wood without any of the domestic offices required by Kenton estate agents – garage, utility room and french window leading to attractive conservatory – that my mother's eyes were opened to horizons much wider than North London suburbia. But that is her part of the story. We have come to see Great-Aunt Robins who will put us on the trail of our English connections.

We ring the bell. Was the Victoria-plum tree in the front or the back of the house, I whisper to my mother. We wait, ring again and then, after a long pause, we hear slow footsteps coming towards the front door. Great-Aunt Robins does indeed look like a great-aunt now. Tall, gaunt, transparent skin stretched tight over a bony face, white-haired and very nearly blind, she leads us down a narrow gloomy hall lit by one twenty-watt light bulb. Will I pour the tea, she asks; she can still just about manage to do it but she will probably make a bit of a mess. Yes, she can guess why we have come. She has been landed with the role of McHarg Family Chronicler. She has a family tree which she regularly updates. They are all there, the Canadian, American, Australian and Irish cousins. There are also photographs which she hasn't been able to sort out properly because of her failing vision. My nearest relative, of course, says Great-Aunt Robins, is Neville, the retired naval commander living with his wife Heather on the Isle of Wight.

I longed to see the family tree. I wondered if there were in fact two trees, just like the two versions of *Lady Chatterley's Lover*, one censored and one with the dirty bits left in, the first to bring out at Christmas for the official family, the second only for when William Thomas Townley came round and they knew they would not be disturbed.

If my mother had not been there I should, like the professional reporter that I am, have lunged straight into searching questions about the Burmese connection. Frankly, Miss Robinson, what did you really think about us? Tell me, Miss Robinson, what did your uncle tell you about his Burmese mistress? What did the rest of the family think, where did we stand, if anywhere at all, with Dolly and Nancy and Sybil and Amy and Jock? But of course I didn't. I would come back on my own later and try again. In front of my mother such sensitive topics would have been as inappropriate as a discussion about blue films with the vicar's wife. And besides, we had other family business to discuss – hereditary blindness.

This is the reason that had brought us to England. My sister, aged six, was going blind. The best medical treatment, mother was advised by the specialist she consulted in Rangoon, was to be found in London. But Moorfields and Harley Street hadn't been able to do any better. It was a genetic condition, they said, almost certainly hereditary. My parents denied the charge, insisting that there was no blindness on either side of the family. Now, watching Great-Aunt Robins moving carefully around the house, feeling for the bottom step of the hall staircase with her shoe, patting her fingers gently across the table-cloth to the edge of her saucer and then softly up the side of the cup to the handle, the mystery was solved. Oh yes, she said, it was some strange disease of the retina. Several members of the family in Australia and California had it too.

My sister had lost all her sight by the time she was twelve. When we came to England she was enrolled in a school for partially sighted children in Exeter but they said her condition was too advanced and sent her to a school for the blind. I too have always had bad eyes, but my condition was more erratic, remaining more or less stable for years and then suddenly taking a dive ten years ago. Being blind didn't stop my sister going to university, doing VSO, becoming chief medical social worker in a large hospital, marrying and having three children. If I could hold out like Great-Aunt Robins it wouldn't be so bad.

So we talk about retinitis pigmentosa and steer clear of any reference to what the family think of their coloured relations or what Evelyn Sarah's strange half-life with my grandfather was like or even the first time my Great-Aunt Robins saw my father Morny, her cousin from Burma. I know the story well. It is one my father is fond of telling. He has a very distinctive, a very Burmese way of speaking English. It takes him a long time to formulate precisely what he is going to say. You have to be patient while the mental cogs and levers work away, grinding his thoughts into measured speech. He doesn't waste words; when they do come they are clipped, the phrases staccato. It sounds very foreign, very oriental. It was his way of speaking English more than anything else that drove my sensitivie, ambitious, ruthless mother up the wall. Theirs was an acrimonious divorce which has not improved over the years.

'McHarg,' she always called him by his surname, 'McHarg never learned to speak English properly,' she would say with scorn. 'It used to infuriate me. There were some words he could never ever get right, no matter how many times he said them. Like froth. He said *throth* or *throf*. And there was another one. Instead of saying "Take that piece of string and pull it taut", he would say "Pull it taunt". Ugh, I couldn't stand it, I just couldn't stand it.' And my mother grits her teeth and clenches her fists with frustration.

She also couldn't stand the way when he was sitting down he would jiggle one leg up and down, up and down as he spoke, or scratch the inside of his thigh absent-mindedly. 'Just like a bloody coolie,' she said.

I don't believe I've ever heard my father attempt to say froth or taut, or variations of either. There must have been other more substantial grounds than verbal incompatibility for her divorcing him. It was harder, much harder in the 'fifties to get out of a marriage, and what did it was good old-fashioned adultery, my mother having run off with my father's English boss. But we shall come to that by and by.

My father is telling me about the time he first met Great-Aunt Robins. When we left Burma my father was working for a trading company called Steel Brothers. His father had got him the job through the old boys' network. It must have been in 1948 or '49 that the Burmese family McHarg – Morny, Marjorie and the two children, Jennifer and Susan – shut the door of their nice curved bay-windowed house in Christchurch Avenue, got into their new red Morris convertible and drove out to Teddington for tea with Great-Aunt Robins. My mother had bought the car before my father arrived. She was very proud of it. I've seen pictures of the two of them in it, looking like a late entry for the London to Brighton Rally, and fascinatingly exotic. My father was a good-looking man, still is, darker than my mother, tall for a Burmese, broad-shouldered with a high forehead, keen eyes that look steadily into yours and a wide, expressive mouth. My mother was, still is, stunning. Small and graceful with a heart-shaped face, high cheek-bones, wide-set dark eyes, not remotely slitty or even almond-shaped, as oriental eyes are so often called to make them sound more appealing. Only her tiny stature and her delicacy mark her out as oriental. From her face you might place her somewhere in Eastern Europe. What she always had, in those early photographs, is glamour. Her dazzling smile, the way she held her head, her shining swept-back hair are pure Hollywood pin-up stuff. I took her to some Burma Association reunion lunch the other day. Someone said, 'Isn't that Marjorie Lloyd over there? You remember Marjorie Lloyd, the very beautiful one who was at teachers' training college with Dolly Corrie . . .'

To Teddington, then, for tea, this interesting little family from Burma, and my mother takes the children in first while my father parks the car. There is a pause in the narrative. My father's mental machinery is working out the next part of the story. Something he remembers is making him smile.

He crosses one leg over the other, slaps his knee, scratches his thigh and laughs.

'You know, my girl,' (he calls me 'my girl' when he's feeling cheery) 'it's a funny thing, I shall never forget it, your Aunt Robins was talking to your mother but she must have had her eyes glued on the door waiting to set them on me for the first time. I could see the way it was. I could see she was just waiting for this moment and then I came through the door and she said, "I knew it. I knew he would be tall. William told me he was tall but I thought all Burmese were short and so I imagined you would be too. But here you are so straight and so tall." She was very pleased, my girl, very happy.' Presumably Great-Aunt Robins had feared that those mysterious oriental genes might be stronger than the McHargs', and now she was agreeably surprised. My tall, broad-shouldered father coming through the door jingling his car keys must have lifted her spirits, reassuring her that in everything, even inches, the white race is superior.

But the truth is exactly the opposite to what my Great-Aunt Robins supposed. My grandfather with those three impressively reverberating Christian names was a titch. Remember the wedding photograph, William standing, Essie sitting in the wicker chair? The photographer was finding a tactful way to prevent Essie looming over her new husband. He must have been well below average height, remarkably so because when I later ask Neville's wife Heather what her father-in-law was like, the first thing she says is, 'Short, very, very short.' She adds, *sotto voce* (Neville has slipped out of the room for a moment to search for some photographs), that she didn't actually care for him very much. 'Why not?' I say. This is the first criticism I've heard about my grandfather. My father worships him, Neville is cautious, and I don't get another chance to talk to Great-Aunt Robins. But the odds are that, if she couldn't admit that he was small, she would hardly admit to more seriously undesirable characteristics. 'Tell me more,' I whisper to Heather before Neville comes back. 'Well he was very pleased with himself, you know, cocky. And another thing. He once took my mother into the bedroom and showed her rude pictures.'

So why didn't my father put Aunt Robins right then and there? Why didn't he sit down, accept his cup of tea and his chocolate biscuit and say, 'As a matter of fact Auntie, it is my mother who should take the credit for my height. You're right about the Burmese being short and dumpy but you see my mother wasn't Burmese.'

This was news to me, too, but my grandmother was a Shan. She came from one of the many hill tribes that wander freely back and forth across frontiers selling their wares at local markets. The Shans, from the Shan States on the Chinese border, are tall. Even by Shan standards my grandmother was a tall woman. A couple of summers ago I had a surprise visit from Burmese McHarg relatives living in Australia. They brought me letters and pictures and decorative tea towels of New South Wales and two portraits of my grandparents.

It was the first time I had seen my grandmother, Ma Nu. She looks amazing, not beautiful but striking, especially that cool, confident, liberated, very un-Burmese look she has in her eyes. Now I know why. Yes indeed I have done well to get myself a white man, that confident gaze is saying, but see what a very small white man he is. He has given me status, certainly, and a home and jewels but for my part I have given him not only sons but tall sons. We are equal after all.

It is time to pursue the English connection further. Uncle Neville and his wife Heather are waiting at Ryde Pier Head on the Isle of Wight. They couldn't be anything else but English, the sort of English I crave to be part of. Not flashy hooray, or aggressively intellectual, or confusingly

arty, or depressingly worthy, just decent, solid, respectable bridge-playing, garden-loving, *Daily Telegraph*-reading
English. Uncle Neville wears a grey top coat, a V-necked jersey, grey shirt and blue tie. Heather has a tweed skirt, green
cardigan and brogues. They could only be a retired naval
officer and a daughter of the late Colonel. I've brought Tom,
my ten-year-old son, with me. It's the summer holidays.
I can hear Neville who politely offered me the front seat
asking Tom, in that serious, straightforward, man-to-man
way that English people have, how he was getting on at
school.

Meanwhile I am talking to Heather, who is the easiest,
friendliest person in the world, about her childhood in
India. Her father was a colonel in the British Army stationed
in Kasauli on the next ridge to Simla. It was famous for
being home to the Pasteur Institute and the only place to go
if you needed a rabies injection. I should like to quiz Heather
about her own family's view about coloured relations. There
wouldn't have been any dark secrets in her family. Colonel
McNair, like most of the British Army in India, had his
family with him. Heather grew up unconcerned, even
unaware that she was surrounded by coloured faces.

'I remember looking out of the window (we were living
in Pakistan at the time, I must have been about five) and
seeing a European walking down the street. I thought how
very strange and out of place he looked,' said Heather.

She is the sort of woman I could talk to all day. She has
that delightful talent for dropping great events of history
into her conversation and relating them to her family as
if she were talking about going down to Sainsbury's. Like
the earthquake in Quetta in 1926. 'Oh yes,' she says,
'my father managed to buy a whole lot of carpets cheap
after the Quetta 'quake. They were earthquake damaged,
slightly burnt I think.' Like the Russian Revolution. 'You
know that red tea service we've got somewhere, Neville? I

don't bring it out much but it's here somewhere. My mother bought it off some white Russians who were fleeing from the Bolsheviks, poor things. They'd come down through Armenia and Afghanistan and were having to sell off all their possessions as they went. By the time they reached India they were on their uppers. It's rather a nice tea set, we should use it more often.'

Uncle Neville (I always call him Uncle Neville in my head. I like to think that this is because I am showing respect in true Burmese fashion but I suspect it is more likely that craving I have to be related to a genuine hundred per cent Englishman), Uncle Neville is a slight man with a thin, tanned face and sad eyes which remain melancholy even when he laughs which he does a lot. Softly, his shoulders shaking slightly as if he is having a private joke with himself. Maybe he is. Heather, whom I have never thought of calling Auntie, is a large, friendly soul who, as the saying goes, speaks as she finds. I can imagine her telling her friends at the bridge table about the time Neville's niece came to visit him without the slightest embarrassment. They moved to Bembridge from Datchet in the 'fifties. Dartmouth, Simla, Datchet, Bembridge. How blissfully English it all sounds, like places that characters in a Terence Rattigan play might talk about. I'm beginning to feel a little light-headed. This is my real half-uncle who fits as snugly into the English establishment as the knitted cosy on the teapot. Not once has he asked me where I come from or told me how fascinatingly exotic I must feel. I shall have to be careful that I am not being lulled into a sense of false security and tomorrow when the woman at the bus-stop asks the old question 'Where are you from?' because of Uncle Neville I might reply rudely 'From London, of course. Why do you ask?'

The McHargs live in a solid, unshowy house built in the 'fifties. Neville says there is something interesting about either the house or its architect but I'm not listening and anyway Heather is talking over him. She does occasionally. Slamming the car door behind her she says that the house is called Wilbercote, one of those silly hybrid names made up by the people who first lived there. 'They were called Wilfred and Beryl. We could have changed it, I suppose, but it's considered unlucky to change the name of houses isn't it?' says Heather. Is it? That must be an English superstition.

In Burma it would be considered unlucky to pee against the side of the house because it would upset the *nyat* or spirit of Wilbercote. Every house in Burma has a resident *nyat*, every pagoda, every shrine, every tree, every bush – everything in fact that needs protection has a guardian spirit. Burmese *nyats* have beautiful names like the Lady with the White Umbrella, the Prince with the Green Slippers, and the Laughing Woman with the Water Melon. Close to where my Uncle Johnny lives in Rangoon there is a house whose relatively new *nyat* is called Major Thompson. *Nyats* have to be constantly cajoled, appeased and bribed with presents of fruit or flowers or prayers. This way they will take their duties as guardians seriously. If there is nothing for it but to pee against the side of the house, then a muttered *Kador kador*, meaning Forgive me, please forgive me, should deflect any malevolent intentions. *Kador kador* are the first Burmese words I learnt, to be said when English people say 'Touch wood' or 'Fingers crossed' when you walk under ladders or see a lone magpie or open a birthday present three days early.

Tom and I have been invited for lunch. Heather has made that very English sort of salad with everything on separate plates for you to assemble yourself. There are hard-boiled eggs cut into quarters on one, pieces of tomato on another, sliced cucumbers on a saucer, sticks of celery in a glass, a bowl of undressed salad and a bottle of Heinz salad cream.

It's all very friendly and polite. I fancy Uncle Neville is giving me furtive glances; I don't blame him. Last time he saw me was forty years ago when his father met my mother, my sister and me off that troop-ship in Liverpool and took us back to the bungalow in Windermere to stay with his wife for a couple of days. Does he remember, I ask. Not really he says and disappears into another room, returning with a handful of old photographs. He found them in a trunk in the attic of his parents' house when he was clearing up their effects. They both died in 1949. Maybe I know some of these people, this rather attractive woman for instance and these two little girls? Of course I know them. The two little girls standing stiff and smiling in baggy white winceyette knickers in front of a rockery are my sister and myself in the back garden of 34 Christchurch. It was the perfect garb for sunbathing and paddling when we went to Margate for summer holidays. For some reason we never owned bathing costumes. And the rather attractive woman with the film-star smile and swept-back hair is my mother in her uniform as a junior officer in the WACI, the Women's Army Corps India. We laugh awkwardly and Heather suggests a walk on the beach before tea and the ferry back to Portsmouth.

We stroll along a pebble beach. The wind is whipping up grey, grubby-looking waves. Heather asks Tom if he wouldn't like a quick dip, she swims all through the summer months. Tom says politely but firmly that he thinks perhaps he'll give it a miss today. Heather looks disappointed. I feel we've let her down. We have not inherited the McHarg stamina, the fighting spirit that determined Neville to take a stand against his father and insist on going to Dartmouth. Neither have we that native fortitude that compels the English to peel off their clothes on a cold, windy, sunless afternoon and thrash about in sea water full of bobbing debris.

We return to Wilbercote for tea. They must come and visit us in our cottage near Petworth one day, it's so convenient on the Portsmouth line. What about Sunday lunch in a couple of months before the children go back to school? So they come and my mother is there and Heather, who must be nearly seventy, borrows a swimsuit and plunges into our inflatable four-foot-deep children's swimming pool which impresses everyone for it is another cold, windy, sunless afternoon. It is all very friendly and polite but now I have come to the Isle of Wight on my own. There is no excuse, no *pas devant les enfants*, no mother whose sensibilities might be affronted. I want to ask Neville what he really felt about his coloured relations and what his father told the English family about them.

Uncle Neville says that actually it wasn't such a rare thing actually, I mean Europeans working out East actually and forming an association with people out there. He uses the word actually as other people say 'er' or 'um' sometimes three or four times in a single sentence. I like it. I find it very English. There was a plummy girl at university with me called Gloria Bolingbroke Kent. She went hunting and knotted her headscarf so tightly on her chin she had difficulty speaking, yet she could still say 'absolutely fantastic actually' as one syllable.

'But what did your father say about our lot?' I persist.

'Well actually I didn't ask him. I took the line that it was none of my business. And anyway I didn't know my father very well,' says Neville. 'First time I met him I must have been about seven. He came home after the war. All I remember about the visit is that he and my mother had to go to France because my grandfather who ran an English school in Boulogne had just died.' Next time Neville saw his father was in 1926 when there was the controversy about Dartmouth.

'Why didn't your father want you to go to Dartmouth?'

I asked. 'Was it just the extra expense?' It says something about Neville's attitude to his father that as soon as he'd saved up £100 from his naval salary he offered to make up for the extra expense the college fees had cost his father by buying the old man shares in a promising new public company called Imperial Chemical Industries. That was in 1934.

'I really don't know, actually,' says Neville. 'It must have been my height. He was worried I'd be too small for the Navy.'

The height factor seems to be an obsession with William Thomas Townley who had taken a Shan giantess to his bed. I didn't want to hear any more about height. I wanted to hear about us. Did Uncle Neville know about us when he went to Dartmouth? 'Yes,' he said. 'My brother told me.' But he couldn't remember how they found out. Neville clearly wasn't enjoying this. 'Maybe it was something I heard my mother discussing with Lady Ireland.'

This was the first time I heard about Essie's impressive family and Neville's grandfather, General Sir Robert Ireland, who was Number Three in the British Army before being killed in an accident on Portsmouth station. 'Goodness, what happened?' I heard myself saying, but I wasn't listening. I was feeling slightly dizzy, but at the same time I could not get out of the corner of my mind the incongruous ghost of my own maternal step-grandfather Ko Ko sitting cross-legged on his Chinese carpet in Taunggyi, a big cheroot sticking out of his mouth, counting his ten-rupee notes with his go-downs on the river full of onions and hides and *stik lak* (lacquer). The daft thing is that Ko Ko would probably have been as delighted with Sir Robert and Lady Ireland as I was. My mother too. I can hear her dropping it deftly into bridge small talk.

'He fell under a train actually,' says Neville.

'What? Sorry, who?' I say, coming back to Wilbercote and beef casserole.

'General Sir Robert,' says Uncle Neville. 'It was all in the papers. He fell under a train on Portsmouth station in 1920-something.'

No, of course it isn't funny that a distinguished soldier, with heaven knows how many medals, who survived Mafeking and Lucknow and for all I know Sebastopol, should lose his footing on Portsmouth station. It's just that falling accidentally under trains is what natives in the Burmese jungle unfamiliar with modern transport are far more likely to do.

So Neville went to Dartmouth and it was no doubt in those whispered conversations between his mother and Lady Ireland that they decided it was better to keep mum at his new school about the coloured relations. You never knew, it might count against him when it came to promotion.

'Is that what your mother felt?' I asked. 'Did she and your father ever talk about the Burmese McHargs, about my father?'

'I don't know actually, well actually I can't really say,' says Uncle Neville unhappily and then, from looking down at the table at the remains of his beef stew, he suddenly seems to come to a decision. He looks up and says, 'Look here, do you really need to write this book? I mean, actually, it's going to hurt a lot of people actually.'

I know it is. I've been thinking that myself. I have been thinking that it might have been kinder to wait until my parents weren't around because it is bound to hurt them too. Trouble is if I do wait till then I won't be able to check if I've got things right. Now I can pick up the phone and say, 'Mum, you know that girl you swapped a matchbox with at school for five rubies remember, was her name Nancy Wemyss or Beryl Stone?'

'So why are you doing it?' says Uncle Neville. And I'm trying to work it out when Heather, who has left the table to bring in mince pies and coffee, comes to my rescue.

'Because it's interesting, that's why,' she says over her shoulder. 'It's like finding a suitcase full of interesting things you never realised you had.'

'But couldn't you write it as a novel and change everyone's names? I mean I don't think Andrew knows about any of this,' protests Neville. Andrew is their son in his mid-forties.

'Look,' I try to explain, 'it's because I've got this complex about being half-Burmese. It's because I look the way I do that I've had this rather odd sort of life. I'm trying to find out why.'

'But you don't look different,' insists Uncle Neville. 'If I passed you in the road I wouldn't think there was anything different about you.' His voice is pleading. He is doing a good job for the defence but it won't wash. I'm afraid I do look foreign and it has made a difference, I say. Even now when we're all so liberal and liberated and aware. And then, to make him understand my point of view a little better, I tell him about Sir Adrian Boult.

'You mean the great conductor,' says Heather.

Yes that's the one, the great conductor. It happened not long after I joined the *Observer* back in the early 'seventies. David Astor is the editor. I've been taken on as a stand-in for Polly Toynbee who has gone off to write a book about working women. I'm on the 'Pendennis' column. Sir Adrian is conducting the LSO. I forget the news peg, maybe it's a new season, maybe it's a new symphony. Whatever it is, the diary editor feels that an interview with the conductor would be interesting. I'm about to start the usual string of contact telephone calls when our music critic wanders in. Sir Adrian, he says, has a legendary secretary, a veritable dragon whose life's ambition is to keep her master away from the Press. 'Here's his home number,' says the music critic. 'Don't say where you got it. He's a decent old stick, just hen-pecked by his wife and his secretary.'

I telephone Sir Adrian, explain my mission and he *is* a decent old stick. Certainly he will talk to me for a few minutes or so during a rehearsal break at the Royal Festival Hall. We make a date. I arrive at the stage door, explain my presence to the stage door keeper and am shown into the Green Room. I can hear the orchestra next door. I'm five minutes early. A woman in a blue coat and one of those close-fitting felt hats is sitting by the door knitting.

'Who are you?' she says. She does not look friendly.

'I've come to interview Sir Adrian Boult,' I say.

'But you don't have an appointment,' she says, putting down her knitting.

'Yes I do, I spoke to him last night and he agreed to see me,' I say.

'Impossible, I am his secretary and I know nothing about this,' says Madame Defarge. 'This is highly irregular. All his interviews are made through me.'

'I'm sorry but he said I should come and see him during rehearsal break,' I say.

'We'll see about that,' says the dragon getting to her feet. The orchestra has stopped playing. I can hear chairs being scraped back and muffled conversation. Before I can pass her the dragon has hurried ahead and when I arrive she and the conductor are deep in conversation. I wait.

At length the Great Conductor turns and stalks past me. 'Hello, I'm from the *Observer*,' I begin. 'You agreed to give me ten minutes of your time during the break.'

'I did nothing of the kind,' snaps the Great Conductor. 'I don't know what you mean by barging in here without proper authority.' The musicians have paused in their packing up and are listening to this exchange with interest. I remind Sir Adrian of our telephone conversation the previous day but he is becoming more and more agitated. And irate. I can see the dragon listening from the Green Room doorway. 'I must ask you to leave immediately,' shouts the Great Conductor. 'This is really too much. Please go immediately. I'm a very busy man. I have work to do. I cannot be interrupted. Please leave at once.' So I do.

Uncle Neville has started to laugh softly. 'Quite right, quite right. I'd have done the same myself,' he says.

I stop in mid-sentence, startled. 'But why?' I ask blankly.

'Because you were interrupting the rehearsal, as he said,' says Uncle Neville.

'But I made an appointment with him, I didn't just barge in,' I say.

'Don't be silly Neville. She spoke to the man, don't you understand?' Heather has now joined in.

'Oh I see,' says Uncle Neville. But he is still laughing. I can see his thin shoulders shaking under his jersey.

I carry on, not quite as confidently as before. Uncle Neville's quivering shoulders the other side of the table are disconcerting. I leave the Festival Hall rehearsal room. I can hear some of the musicians laughing. 'Sorry, no interview,' I tell the diary editor. 'Nonsense, write it just the way it happened,' he says. 'It will make a funny last paragraph.' And it does. The tale of the Dragon, the Great Conductor and the Hapless Young Reporter. The diary editor gives it a witty headline, CONDUCT UNBECOMING.

First thing Tuesday morning (Sunday newspapers don't work Mondays) the diary editor is summoned to David Astor's office. A hand-delivered letter from Sir Adrian Boult is lying on his desk. I never saw the letter and can only pass on what was subsequently told me. I suspect it was watered down. 'Since when', wrote Sir Adrian, 'has the *Observer* (for which until now I have always had a high regard) started sending wops out as reporters? The one who came to interview me without an appointment couldn't even speak English. It is hardly surprising therefore that the story she wrote was entirely inaccurate and I shall look for an apology in next week's paper.'

Uncle Neville has stopped laughing. He looks confused. Heather is visibly shocked.

'That's absolutely appalling,' she says. 'I hope the *Observer* did nothing of the kind.' Uncle Neville nods vaguely, I hope in agreement.

'No, we didn't. The editor wrote back to Sir Adrian and said if anyone was due an apology it was Miss McHarg and as far as I know that was the end of it.'

There was silence in the kitchen at Wilbercote. Uncle Neville is looking at his mince pie.

'It's all right. Don't worry, I'm quite used to it,' I say, trying to comfort him because he is still looking a bit mixed up. 'When I was on the *Evening Standard* diary they used to call me Kowloon Lucy and if it was raining someone usually said, "Send Sue out to cover that story, she's used to the monsoon."' Uncle Neville smiles uncertainly and to galvanise him into a positive response I tell him that I appreciate that some people are, well, racist really. Not violently so but almost without thinking. I just want to get a reaction from him. By comparison with Uncle Neville, of course, my mother practically qualifies for membership to the Ku-Klux-Klan. She once said new-born Indian babies smell of curry.

I've started something at last. Heather says she cannot understand how people can feel that way. It is very, very wrong. Uncle Neville says that of course he isn't a racist and did I ever hear his story about the dog they had when they were in Pakistan. Uncle Neville spent some time on loan to the Pakistan Navy which he didn't care for, nothing to do with the natives, it was not a good career move that's all. Anyway he and Heather had this dachshund which used once to belong to an Australian posted to Pakistan who didn't want to take the dog back to Australia with him. So Neville said he'd take it and the funny thing was that if a coloured person came into the room the dog would start growling and barking and making a terrible fuss. But if a Pakistani in naval uniform came in the dog was good as gold. 'Extraordinary how the dog could tell the difference, quite extraordinary but there it was.' Then he seems to make up his mind. 'I know intellectually, if I think about it rationally, that there is absolutely no difference between people of different colour. Why should there be? We have the same brains, the same feelings, we're the same. Unfortunately, my heart tells me differently. I just cannot feel the same way about coloured people, I suppose it was the way I was brought up.'

I don't suppose it, I know it. We're back in Windermere with William Thomas Townley and Essie. It is February 1948 and my grandfather has told his wife and son Neville that he is going to Liverpool to collect a Burmese woman and her two children who will be coming to stay for a couple of days. Does he say any more than that? Does he tell them over the tea and Cooper's Oxford Marmalade that the Burmese woman is married to his oldest Burmese son and that the two children are his granddaughters?

'I don't remember very much about it, actually,' says Neville forty years later in Wilbercote on the Isle of Wight. 'I know we had tea in the garden and talked, I think my mother was a little upset.'

Why, oh why wasn't I born with the gift of total recall that Salvador Dali and Lord Boothby claimed. Dali said he could actually remember being in his mother's womb. He said it felt like being a poached egg in a pan, which begs the question how he knew what a poached egg felt like. My mother would believe him. She's a Buddhist. She believes in reincarnation. Salvador Dali was obviously a poached egg in a former incarnation. In his memoirs Lord Boothby says he remembers the bump bump sensation that his pram made when his nanny pushed him aged three months towards Hyde Park every afternoon. I was three when I met my grandfather. It was the one and only meeting (he died the following year and his wife a few months after) and I don't remember anything about it.

Neither, surprisingly, does my mother. She remembers only Essie's unfriendliness, and William Thomas Townley taking her for a walk in the woods by the house. He said when the weather was cold like this and the air crisp and bracing, it reminded him of winters up-country in Burma. How he missed Burma, he said.

'But what do *you* remember about our visit?' I'm asking Uncle Neville. He was thirty-five and must have been on leave, still a bachelor, although just a month before he had taken a fancy to a big jolly redheaded girl at his cousin Marguerite's wedding. Her name was Heather McNair, her father a colonel in the British Army in India.

I don't know when Neville proposed marriage to Heather. It must have been some time after our visit, which is significant. Meeting my mother and her two small children didn't alter that ingrained attitude he confesses to harbouring towards coloured people, and when he went to see his prospective father-in-law to ask for Heather's hand, he felt duty bound to reveal the family secret. The Colonel must have said he could hack it because on the train going home with Heather afterwards he told her about us, too. 'Don't worry,' he said. 'Your father knows and I'm telling you now, rather than have you find out later, maybe from someone who is just wanting to stir up trouble.'

Our arrival at the family bungalow in Craig Walk, Windermere must certainly have stirred things up. The car would have had the lace curtains twitching – Mr McHarg, the distinguished, if small, white-haired old gentleman at the wheel with, 'well I'm not quite sure how to put it, Madge dear, a coloured woman beside him. Attractive? well yes she was attractive, I'll give her that, but nevertheless coloured, distinctly coloured.'

No, no it was nothing like that, says Neville. The neighbours wouldn't have seen anything and, even if they had, everyone was muffled up in coats and hats because it was February and they would hardly have noticed what you looked like. But why on earth were we having tea in the garden in mid-winter for heaven's sake? We must have been freezing to death. Did Essie suggest it? Did we perhaps smell of curry like those wretched dog-Indian babies?

'I don't remember much,' Neville is saying. 'There was this woman and a child I think.'

'Don't be silly, Neville, you're talking to her right now. Sue here was the child and the woman was Majorie whom we met at Sue's cottage for lunch in the summer, don't you remember?'

No, it's no good, Neville cannot equate a child in the garden of the Windermere bungalow with me. He says there was some talk about the child's eyesight and he seems to remember the woman asking for money to pay for an operation.

When I told my mother this she hit the roof. 'I certainly did not ask for money. I had plenty of money when we arrived. We stayed for a month in the Imperial Hotel in Russell Square and took a taxi every morning to Moorfields Eye Hospital.'

In my mind's eye I am listening to my grandfather telling his wife that Morny's little daughter Jennifer has some mysterious eye disease and her mother is bringing her to England to see a specialist. That's probably all he says but Essie, who has watched her husband send letters and money out to the coloured relations for thirty-five years, immediately thinks another bill is looming. And Neville, her darling boy Neville, gets her side of the story.

The other thing my mother remembers about that visit was how often and how extravagantly Essie praised her younger son. When she said Grace before lunch she didn't say, 'For what we are about to receive may the Lord make us truly thankful.' She said, 'For what we are about to receive may we all be grateful to Neville.' She then told everyone how generous her son was, how when he was on active service he sent home oranges and pineapples, the sort of things they couldn't buy at home in austerity Britain. Yes, Neville is his mother's boy and Morny and Johnny and Jimmy and Peter were his father's.

'He was so proud of his Burmese children,' said Uncle Neville suddenly. He was stirring his coffee after lunch in Wilbercote. Especially when any of them won prizes at school or cups for sport.

'But how did you know they won prizes and cups, Uncle Neville?' I said. 'Did he tell you, did he show you photographs?' One of the pictures rescued from my grandfather's attic chest shows his four Burmese boys in shorts and singlets sitting in front of a row of trophies. On the back in pencil is scribbled the occasion. *1920 Government English High School Maymyo. Morny 20, Johnny 18, Peter won the school boxing championship, GEHS came second in all-Burma inter-school championships.*

'No,' says Uncle Neville, 'he didn't tell us. But these things actually sort of actually percolate through.' And that's all he says for the rest of the afternoon, so Heather and I talk about her childhood in India and how sad it was that Great-Aunt Robins should have died so unexpectedly a few months back. She was eighty-seven but everyone expected her to go on for ever.

It's almost time to catch my ferry. On an impulse I ask my uncle if he ever had any wish, any curiosity, to see his half-brother, my father. What an extraordinary pair they would make, nothing, absolutely nothing in common physically, socially, mentally. Here was the retired Commander, reserved, polite, sitting straight-backed on his dining chair, his thin face conveying genteel correctness with every gesture. Last time I saw my father he was lying improbably on a Victorian *chaise longue* he had just had re-upholstered, in the conservatory built on to the back of his Wembley semi where his late second wife used to do home hairdressing. My father suffers from severe arthritis in his legs and has difficulty walking, so puts them up whenever he can to give himself relief. He was sitting back, arms folded high over his chest, his feet in grey socks sticking out from the bottom of a pair of old grey trousers. He didn't look comfortable, he looked forbidding, like an Emperor holding court. Now that his hair is receding his brow is even higher. 'OK my girl,' he said, 'just give my hair a trim, it's getting shaggy.'

Is it into this domestic scene, me cutting my father's hair, the grey tufts falling on to his socks, the bead curtain in front of the garden door hanging slightly crooked, that my Uncle Neville is to appear for that first momentous encounter? No I'm sorry, I can't see it. Neither can he. 'I'm very comfortable here,' he says. 'I think I'm a little too old for surprises.'

The Portsmouth ferry is waiting on Ryde Pier Head. I'm shaking hands and saying thank you and Uncle Neville escorts me to the gate. 'You know,' he says, 'I do remember something very clearly. Whenever a letter arrived from Burma my father was so excited. He called it a red letter day. He would read it over and over again at the breakfast table and then he would lock himself into the study for the rest of the morning so that he could reply.' Uncle Neville looked across the Solent, I don't think he was focusing on Portsmouth. 'At least it gave the rest of us a bit of peace,' he said.

3 ∫

William Thomas Townley

When my grandfather left his five Burmese children and went home to his wife and family in England, their mother, my grandmother, married his chauffeur and had three more children, all boys. There is an old Burmese tradition that when the *phongyis*, the Buddhist monks, come to your door every morning begging for alms, you must take care, as you spoon rice or fish or *balachan* (pickle) into their bowls, that you do not step on their shadows. It will bring bad luck. When the *phongyis* came to our house they took care not to step on my grandmother's shadow out of respect for a woman with seven sons. Women's liberation has a little way yet to go in Burma.

William Thomas Townley was not a saint – I can hear Essie seconding that – but, unlike the majority of his generation, nor was he a chauvinist. Most of the Europeans in the government service were. He did not, as they did, live majestically alone in his large government bungalow next to the Gymkhana Club in Prome, waited on by Burmese cooks, bearers, gardeners, houseboys and verandah *derzis*, while his Burmese mistress and children slummed it in the thatched native quarter down the hill. My grandfather moved Ma Nu, my grandmother, in with him. My father was born in the District Officer's residence, a handsome house, which he refers to as the bungalow, even though it was on two floors and the whole thing on stilts. I've seen photographs of the Prome residence. In one there are two servants in the background dressed in livery with turbans and gold-braided epaulets like greeters in a Mayfair restaurant.

I know nothing about the circumstances in which either of my Burmese grandmothers met their British benefactors. My mother says vaguely that the men were probably just passing through the village on a tour of duty and saw the girls bathing in the river or something. I doubt that very much. I think she's been watching too many Gary Cooper films. Isn't there one when the hero first sees his Red Indian bride splashing about in a secluded creek in New Mexico? I have reservations about the bathing-belle story. For a start the Burmese are a modest race and wouldn't allow their women to uncover themselves in a public place. Even today tourists to Burma have to obey a dress code – no mini-skirts for women or singlets for men. But even if Charlie Lloyd, my mother's father, had spied Ma Shweh Ohn, my grandmother, washing in the river, he wouldn't have seen much. Occasionally in England when people learn about my mother's Burmese roots they invite her to give after-dinner talks to the Rotary Club or the Women's Institute. She will kneel in front of the elaborately carved camphor wood chest she had brought with her from Burma and take out one of the Burmese national costumes she keeps wrapped in tissue paper and mothballs inside. It is very simple. A white embroidered cotton jacket, close fitting, cropped at the waist, with long narrow sleeves. And a *longyi* or sarong of heavy crimson silk, richly embroidered with a wide black cotton band at the top to ensure a firm grip. The high point of my mother's after-dinner talk comes when she tells the audience how cleverly and how modestly Burmese women washed themselves in a stream. There is a low murmur of excited anticipation at this stage. Is this exotic little person going to give the Godalming Townswomen's Guild a strip-tease? My mother will coolly unwind the top of her longyi and then pull it just above her collar-bone where she rewinds and fastens it. 'Like this,' she says. 'That's all they do. Of course they will remove their tops as well and then they just wash themselves underneath.'

I have no idea how William Thomas Townley met Ma Nu, or Miss Tender, the young girl of sixteen or seventeen from the Shan hill tribes. What was she doing as far south as Prome anyway? I know nothing about her family, apart from the fact that she had a brother. My grandfather found him a job in the Forestry Service and he once lost his temper and nearly killed his supervisor. Fiery temper runs in the family. My grandmother had spectacular rows with her second husband, one Abdul Aziz. What a wonderful name I said when my father first told me. Up till then I had been crediting my mother's stepfather Ko Ko with the wherewithal to flutter conventional dovecotes, but how could anyone with another stepfather called Abdul Aziz be taken seriously in polite English society?

'Tell me some more about Abdul Aziz,' I asked my father. 'Wasn't he my grandfather's chauffeur?'

'Certainly not,' said my father, looking shocked. 'He had his own taxi service at Maymyo where we were living when my father went home to England. He used to drive people to Mandalay, forty-two miles away. He had a very smart car, a Whippet Overlander it was called, with his initials in a sort of gold insignia on a brass plate on the driver's door.'

There was scarcely any age difference between Abdul Aziz and my grandmother which my father says is why they had so many rows, sometimes ending with my grandmother throwing all Abdul Aziz's clothes out of the window into the road. My father was then a teenager and remembers defending his mother against his stepfather's retaliatory outbursts. She never ever had arguments with William Thomas Townley whom she called *Thakin*, meaning master. What few feminist tendencies I have winced to hear my tall, proud grandmother calling her little squirt of a bloke master. And then I remembered something. *Thakin . . . thakin*, the word had a familiar ring, it was what my mother called my stepfather David James whenever she wanted to say something private to him and they spoke Burmese together, and in that context it sounded like English people saying 'darling'.

Soon after my father was born, William Thomas Townley transferred north of Mandalay to Mogok where his younger sons were all born. It was a large establishment and quite capable of housing my grandfather and his staff of eight in one half and my mother, the children and two or three less grand servants in the other. I wish I knew more about the intimate details of their domestic arrangements. I have an insatiable and I suspect prurient curiosity about other people's life-styles. You can tell so much about people by what they have on their bathroom shelves and coffee tables. Even if my father could remember his life in Mogok he isn't the type to store the sort of trivial details that I relish. I have to be content with broad brushstrokes.

My grandfather's side of the house had half a dozen reception rooms, the largest being his study overlooking the lawn. In this he had his desk and a handsome teak table set in the window where at four o'clock every afternoon he and my grandmother and the children had traditional English afternoon tea with buttered toast. This was the only meal he shared with them. There were two cooks, my grandfather's man, plus an assistant who prepared steak, roasts and casseroles and similar plain English fare, while in her part of the house Ma Nu's cook served up rice and curry and pickled fish in chillies and oil. The family's midday meal was eaten inside the house, it was too hot to have it anywhere else, but their evening meal would be laid outside on the lawn.

The Burmese eat with their fingers. I used to think that years of practice would have made them expert at doing this neatly, tidily with no messy spillage. This is not the case. I've seen exquisitely delicate Burmese girls, like that portrait of Saw Ohn Nyun the Shan princess, finish a meal of prawn *balachan* and noodles with gravy round their ears. They don't bother with chairs either, preferring to sit on the ground, their legs crossed beneath a low table. It was at such a table on the lawn that my grandmother, my father, my uncles and aunt had their supper every day in Mogok at around six o'clock.

Half-way through the meal my grandfather would come out of the house through the french windows of the study that led on to the verandah. He would be wearing evening dress and carrying a whisky tumbler. He might stop for a moment to admire the six-foot-diameter table he had had hewn from a single piece of wood which occupied pride of place on the wooden deck. It was the envy of his European friends. He would then walk over to chat for a few minutes to my grandmother, or play with the children before strolling down the hill to the Club for the rest of the evening.

Every town had a European club. In Mogok it was called the Gymkhana Club and it had six members, my grandfather, the doctor, the police chief, the bishop, the government officer in charge of the mines and the colonel from the nearby garrison. They took it in turns to be Secretary.

'No women?' I asked.

'I can't remember a single English wife in Mogok,' said my father.

For a change, my grandfather might entertain the club members to dinner at his residence with the table boy and his assistant in their livery. His Burmese family would not be part of this, of course, but my grandfather always introduced Ma Nu and the children to his guests during the pre-dinner drinks. I asked my father what the guests thought of them, did they seem curious, surprised, shocked?

'Why should they be shocked, Susan? Everyone knew my father had a Burmese wife, I think they probably respected him for being so open about it, isn't it.' That's another typically Burmese phrase the equivalent, I suppose, of *n'est ce pas* which my father tends to stick indiscriminately on to the end of sentences. 'He wasn't ashamed of us, my mother was a very attractive woman after all and he was proud to show her off. Why not?'

Openness and pride in Mogok was one thing, but head office in Rangoon were not as indulgent as the members of the Gymkhana Club. My grandfather was never promoted to the top position of Conservator of Forests which he would have been, had he played his cards a little less openly and proudly. Years later, when he retired and used to write for news of his old friends to my father who by then was also in the forestry business, he would ask whatever happened to Barrington or Phillips, or Parker and my father would tell him they were conservators in this or that region and old WTT would write back a little sadly and say, 'By Gosh, all these chaps were my juniors, I taught them the business and look where they are now.'

He may have missed out on promotion, or even a knighthood, but he had a pretty good life in Burma. I'm not sure I like everything I've heard about him. Like the way he insisted on his children greeting him with the *shi-ko*, the traditional Burmese form of respect where you kneel, palms held together in front of your forehead and bow your head to the ground, like in *The King and I*. The Chief Clerk used to bring his children home from school in Maymyo for the holidays, travelling back by the Irrawaddy paddle steamer, and my grandfather would drive from Mogok to meet them. When he stepped on to the boat they would all be expected to bow down on the deck in front of him, with the other passengers watching.

'Tell me some more about this *shi-ko* business,' I asked my father. I hated the idea of my grandfather forcing his children to grovel like that. It had overtones of people putting their pet corgis through tricks for visitors. 'Was it like that?' I said.

'No, no Susan, it wasn't like that at all.' My father pauses for a long time. He's trying to sort the explanation out in his head and it isn't easy. When my father is thinking deeply about something you can practically see the cartoon-style 'thinks' bubble coming out at the side of his head. He bites his lip, narrows his eyes, wrinkles his brow, scratches his thigh and you just have to sit there and be patient. 'It's a Burmese form of behaviour,' he says at last, 'no, not exactly behaviour, wait. I want to put it in a more correct way. It's like paying a sort of homage to your parent, to your superior. It's what you do when you go to the monastery and pray, you kneel down and put your hands together like this.'

'But when you did it to your father did you do it out of fun, were you all giggling together when you knelt down on the deck on the paddle steamer?' I was suddenly remembering a similar exercise at the convent I was dumped in for two years when my mother went out to join my father in Borneo. Most days we spent three hours in chapel but this was nothing compared to Easter when in the three days from Good Friday to Easter Sunday we practically lived in our pews. There was something called the Vigil which began after supper on Good Friday and lasted till well after midnight, starting with us all coming into chapel on our knees. Walking on your knees, particularly for the fat girls, wasn't easy and I can still remember the suppressed giggles as we crashed into each other's backsides, dropping our rosaries and trying not to catch Sister Agnes de Sales's eye. If making a *shi-ko* was anything like that the little McHargs must have thought it a great joke. But my father seventy years on does not think it a joke. In fact he's getting a little angry and red in the face at my flippancy.

'Look Susan, when you are as young as that I don't think you would regard it as fun or a joke or impolite or whatever it is. You do that just because your father tells you to do that – to him or your superiors.'

'So would you do that to a Burmese then?' I want to know.

'No,' says my father. 'A Burmese would do that to me.'

'To *you*? Why, because you're an Anglo-Burmese?'

'No, not because I'm an Anglo, because I'm his boss.'

'So you do it to someone superior in rank, is that it?' I say. I really do want to get to the bottom of this. I can still see Yul Brynner with that evil smirk on his face sitting ever lower and lower on the ground so that poor old Deborah Kerr who has to be always in an inferior position ends up with her nose on the floor.

'No, no Susan. You don't understand. When I was with Steel Brothers, all right, I've got my elephant staff and so on and when they come up for their pay they would give just a little bow, just a polite sort of thing, and I would do that to my father, just because he would like me to do that because it's, you might say, a high standard of behaviour towards your parents, your superiors.' Aha now I get it. Now I twig. It's the same as fathers making their sons call them sir. And, believe it or not, we still know people who do it.

There were other things: I didn't much like the idea of

my grandfather getting that same chief clerk who brought the sons home from school to keep an eye on Ma Nu when he was on home leave in England and when he retired for good. Spying, I call it.

'Just taking care that we were looked after properly,' says my father.

One thing on which WTT was adamant was that his children should be brought up as Christians. It was principally for this reason that all the boys were sent to the Government English High School in Maymyo, which the headmaster, Mr McClean, ran like an English public school. The school houses were called The Templars and The Crusaders, The Argonauts, The Adventurers and St Johns. My father was in St Johns, rising to become deputy head of house. The uniform was light blue and dark blue, representing Oxford and Cambridge, and all the lessons were in English.

So when my grandfather left Burma he instructed his former chief clerk to send him regular reports about the family, together with an annual photograph of the children. Not Ma Nu. I've seen some of these pictures. They're just as you would expect of a formal portrait, the two older boys standing with their arms folded, my Auntie May in her St Michael's Girls' Protestant School uniform in the middle and the younger boys, Peter and Jimmy, at the front on chairs.

Not long after he went home to Essie, the chief clerk had disturbing news to report to WTT. Contrary to all his instructions my grandmother had persuaded my father to make his *shin-pyu*, the Buddhist equivalent of making one's first communion. My father tried to explain its significance to me.

'For every Burmese mother with sons the highest what do you call it, what is that word?'

'Accolade,' I suggest.

'Yes that will do, the highest way to pay respect, the

51 •

highest ambition a mother has is for her son to shave his head and become a monk. By doing that, they claim the son is repaying his mother gratitude equivalent to half her breast. You see, my girl, how it is. You are carried in your mother's womb for nine months at the risk to her life. She breast-feeds you and cares for you because you are her son and if you become a monk that is a great achievement.'

'Greater than being a doctor or lawyer?' I want to know. When it comes to having sons become doctors Burmese mothers are the same as Jewish mothers.

'Far greater than being a doctor or lawyer,' says my father. 'Those are sort of material things, yes? Put it that way if you like, isn't it?'

When my father talks about becoming a monk he doesn't mean permanently, just for six months when the boy is thirteen. They go to the monastery, they have their heads shaved, they wear the traditional saffron robes and they beg for alms. When my grandmother asked my father if he would make his *shin-pyu* he refused. Not just because WTT had worked on him, though my father took his responsibilities as the eldest boy seriously. He was always my grandfather's favourite. There was another reason – the boys at GEHS (most of them staunch Protestants) would laugh at him. No, he told his mother, he wouldn't shave his head and wear saffron. Mr McClean wouldn't like it, his father wouldn't like it and, what was more, his mother knew his father wouldn't like it.

Ma Nu didn't give up. She was canny enough to know that if Morny could be persuaded, then his brothers would follow his example. She did what most mothers bent on getting their own way would have done. She bribed him. She told my father that she would buy him a new bicycle from Rowe & Co., the big department store in Mandalay, and a pair of boxing gloves for Peter if he would just give up half a year to pleasing her and the Lord Buddha.

'Go on Morny,' begged Peter, 'and ask for a football too and a gun so we can go squirrel-shooting with the Barringtons.'

My father gave in. What was a promise to a father you would most likely never see again compared to a new bike and a squirrel-shooter? He shaved his head, he went to the monastery for instruction and a letter spelling out Ma Nu's treachery winged its way to Windermere. That must have been a special kind of red letter day in Craig Walk. I don't suppose for one moment that those particular contents would have percolated through to Neville and Essie. When WTT locked himself into his study to reply to it and give them a bit of peace they would have no idea how unpeaceful the old man was feeling.

'What happened? Did he stop sending you money?' I asked my father. It was a bit of a risk for Ma Nu to take with five small children to support, though I think at this stage she'd already taken up with Abdul Aziz and the Whippet Overlander. The incident also belies some of the stories my mother has told me about her mother-in-law which, even allowing for the natural antipathy between every new wife and her mother-in-law, seem a bit strong.

'Miss Tender? Miss Devil more like.' My mother firmly believed that Ma Nu was a witch. When my sister was born in Prome in 1941 and Ma Nu came to see her first grandchild my mother placed lemons all round the house and especially under pillows to ward off witchcraft (an old Burmese remedy). She also said that Ma Nu was scheming and money grabbing and that when my father was working for Steel Brothers in Rangoon, Ma Nu walked into the Accounts Office and demanded his monthly wage cheque which, she claimed, was her rightful due. I told my father this story.

'Your mother is lying again,' he said. 'How could my

mother have taken my money? I had a salary paid in every month to the bank.'

Both my parents have a distinct way of saying the word 'salary'. It isn't just the pronunciation, as in sal'ry without the second 'a', it is the reverential tone, almost a whisper they adopt when they say it. Salaries were what the British paid their British employees. Dog-Indians and poor Burmese, without the benefit of a missionary school education, got wages.

Paying the monthly wages to his household is one of my father's most vivid memories of his father. It was one of the highlights of the children's lives. They would run, laughing and talking, into the big room and crowd round the table by the window where afternoon tea was served. This was early morning before WTT went to work. All the house servants would line up in front of the desk in order of seniority. First the cook, then the table boys, next their assistants, then the *amah*, the children's nanny, then the *syce*, the Indian groom who looked after my grandfather's two horses, and then the *mali* the lowest servant whose chores included sweeping and emptying the thunderboxes, as they were taught to call the lavatories. My grandfather would take down a huge ledger from the shelf behind the desk and make a great show of looking up each servant's record, seeing what he had been paid last month, what he was owed this month. It was always the same, so the preamble was purely to make the occasion more dignified and important, and then he would unlock the tin cash box, count out their money and hand it over. After each transaction the servant would *shi-ko* and move a couple of paces to the left and the next account would be settled.

What else does my father remember about his childhood? There were the afternoons when WTT took the children walking in the forest behind the house with the two horses. He had had a track made for riding. One of the horses was frisky, the other docile. William Thomas Townley rode the charger, allowing the children to take turns on the other. One afternoon they were engaged in this wholly pleasant pastime and it was my Auntie May's turn on the horse. She must have been about ten at the time. My father, telling the story once again, laughs out loud at the memory. He does actually say 'Ho, ho' when he laughs.

'So there we all were, my girl, in the forest with the horses when suddenly, ho, ho, a bee stings the horse May is riding and ho, ho, ho, off it goes. Bolts, no one can stop it, not my father, not the *syce* and there's poor May holding on to the neck and screaming. Ho, ho. How we all laughed.'

William did not laugh when he found trespassers. My father remembers him chasing after peasants who had crept in for firewood, yelling at them to get off his land. I think his bark was worse than his bite. The locals called him *guang phyn thakin gyi* which means big white boss. He wasn't that old. He was forty-nine when my father was born and retired at sixty. This was late for someone working in the tropics. My stepfather who was also in Forestry in Burma and Borneo retired when he was forty-eight, but that may have been because he too had blotted his copy-book by running off with an Anglo-Burmese.

Getting information about my father's childhood is an exercise in patience. Like most elderly people his memory is selective. Certain anecdotes he remembers so clearly that it's as if he's reading a script, he uses exactly the same phrases, the same pauses, the same inflections – the one about the first time he met Great-Aunt Robins for instance. Infuriatingly, for a would-be biographer like me, certain aspects of his early life are blank. The relationship, for instance, between his parents. Every time I try and pin him down on how they behaved to each other, what they said, where they went, he says he can't remember. And if I persist with the questions, he becomes irritated.

'What do you mean, Susan? Of course they got on together. Why not? They stayed together for fifteen years, isn't it.'

I once asked him if WTT ever showed he felt anything for Ma Nu, if he ever put his arm round her or even kissed her. My father said tetchily that the Burmese didn't and still don't go in for public displays of emotion. In Burma a wife does not necessarily love her husband but she respects him, she cares for him and she is loyal. 'As for kissing and canoodling in public, that's what your Western couples and so forth go in for isn't it,' says my father with scorn.

It's interesting that *nun deh* which is the Burmese for 'give me a kiss', actually means 'give me a sniff'. How unerotic can you get! But then I never think of the Burmese, men or women, as being particularly sexy. They're far too passive, too gentle, too detached to associate with the sort of earthiness that goes with raw sex. Nothing could be more alien to those smooth-faced china-doll Burmese girls with their eyes demurely downcast and one small bird-boned hand pressed against their mouths to stifle the inevitable giggle (all the Burmese girls I met in Burma giggled), than a fleshy, wet, open-mouthed, lip-grinding Hollywood kiss. A quick, clinical sniff, the kind my mother often gives to decide whether a pillowcase needs washing, is far more appropriate.

So what do I know for sure about the relationship between my grandfather and Ma Nu? They shared a house but kept strictly to their own quarters. My grandfather had his own bedroom but married couples in those days often did. They took their meals separately, they didn't touch each other, or show any physical affection for each other in public. Nor, as far as my father can recall, did they have what we would call one-to-one conversations or soul-searching discussions about the meaning of life, as my generation of liberated wives and mothers have been taught to expect. They laughed together a lot. The incident with the bee in the forest and poor little May screaming her head off on a bolting horse would have kept them going for weeks.

If I'm being realistic I can hear them both having private, nationalistic jokes about each other, William Thomas Townley confiding to the English doctor at the Club that some of Ma Nu's homespun remedies for ailments were positively primitive. She had, for instance, a horse-shoe-shaped piece of wood which, placed at the back of the neck resting against a certain point, could relieve a headache. And ā favourite cure for snake bite was to cut the tail off the snake and swallow it immediately. I can hear everyone at the Gymkhana Club having a good laugh about that and maybe the Colonel offering to buy the next round of Harry Squeezers on the strength of it.

And then I tiptoe into my grandmother's side of the house where the children are tumbling around on the floor, maybe playing an indoor version of a stick-and-ball game called *gille dundoo*. Here's how it works. You put a piece of wood on the edge of a stool, hit it with another and try and hit it again before it hits the ground. The stationary stick is the *gille*, the stick used as a bat is the *dundoo*. While the boys are playing this May, the oldest, is probably helping her mother pound spices with a stone pestle or maybe they're putting *thanaka* on their cheeks. This is a powder made out of sandalwood, a bit like Max Factor Pan stick. A couple of Ma Nu's friends have come up from the village to have green tea and peanuts and chat and Ma Nu is making them giggle hugely by telling them about William's extraordinary vegetable garden. Everyone in Mogok knows about Mr McHarg's rose garden. It is the pride of the town. He has had rose plants sent out from England and tends his Enid Harkness and Peace as lovingly as his two gardeners do. Ma Nu likes the roses, the Burmese love flowers but cannot quite get the hang of people going out of their way to create flower gardens. Wild flowers in Burma are so profuse that to plant a formal flower garden is a bit like seeding daisies and dandelions.

So when William said he was going to make a vegetable garden Ma Nu was enthusiastic. Here was a really worthwhile project. She approved of the earthworks. She may even have offered a rare opinion about the positioning of the terraces. The ideal spot was the steep slope behind the house but it had to be terraced first to accommodate the seed beds. Ma Nu was probably able to advise on the traditional irrigation system of running the water through bamboo conduits from terrace to terrace and then into lengths of perforated split bamboo hoses. But instead of planting the sort of vegetables Ma Nu was familiar with, okra and *brinjal* and corn, once again William sent to England for seeds and planted in Ma Nu's eyes the strangest imaginable things, carrots and cabbage and cauliflowers and, most singular of all, small, bitter, tightly wrapped leaf balls called Brussels sprouts which his cook would boil and boil until they were soft. Her visitors would sip their tea, smooth their *longyis* over their knees, as they sat cross-legged on the floor, and try to imagine what a carrot or a cauliflower could look like.

Upon which my grandmother would suggest a walk round the cabbage patch and tiny brown hands pressed against their mouths to smother any giggles, they would adjourn to the garden. What else might Ma Nu have found amusing and strange about her partner? His endless changes of clothes probably, a different uniform to suit every social occasion; the casual blazer he put on for tea, his dinner-jacket for the Club, his riding habit, his Sunday suit for going to church. Three *longyis* which folded into small squares which could fit comfortably into a Shan bag and the same number of shirts, one white for formal wear, would be all the requirements of a Burmese.

But the best joke of all was the new assistant district officer, a young Englishman who had moved into the house down the road. Rumours of his coming had preceded him, most especially the news that he was a bachelor. The conversation in the thatched houses in the village at the bottom of the hill was full of excited speculation. Which local beauty would snap this one up? And then the new assistant district officer arrived from England, fresh-faced, awkward in a horse-drawn tonga full of packing cases. A small crowd of locals formed a welcoming party at the top of the drive leading to his residence, anxious for a good look. But wait, who was that fierce-looking woman with him? His mother. She was taking no chances with her son's health and happiness. She had come to be his housekeeper and sole companion.

My grandfather must have known that some of his English eccentricities made Ma Nu laugh. He liked to hear her laugh. He deliberately exaggerated his quirkiness to amuse her and give her something to giggle about with her friends. In the rainy season, for instance, when it was too wet to play outside or go riding in the forest he would burst into the children's room and say 'Come on everyone, exercise. It's unhealthy to sit around, you must have proper exercise. Follow me.' And then he would march round the house, in and out of rooms with the children behind him imitating everything he did. It was the Edwardian equivalent of aerobics. Up and down, up and down he would pump his outstretched arms, left right, left right, he would goose-step along the corridors, one two, one two, he would shout executing starfish jumps, and Morny and Johnny and Jimmy and Peter and sometimes even big sister May would copy him, tears of laughter streaming down their faces, while their mother and the *amah* and the *mali*, and the houseboys watched in amazement.

Twice a year in the cold season my grandfather went on tour in his capacity as District Forest Officer. For the family it was like going on holiday and when twenty years later my grandfather took my mother for a walk in Windermere and told her how much he missed Burma it was probably the memories of those tours of duty that were uppermost in his mind. Imagine the cliché picture of a family about to set off on holiday, everyone running about with bags, an estate car with all its doors open standing outside, and the children begging to be allowed to bring a favourite toy. Substitute four elephants for the estate car, add a dozen excited servants and some pretty large pieces of luggage and you have some idea of the McHargs of Mogok getting ready. Each tour lasted between four and six weeks which sounds long but a vast distance had to be covered, and pack elephants only travel up to ten miles a day, starting at sunrise and stopping at around eleven, before the sun gets too hot. The purpose of these tours of inspection was to see which trees were ready for felling and as well as his household staff my grandfather took half a dozen clerical and technical staff. It must have been so exciting for the children, watching the elephants being loaded up with all the necessary paraphernalia to keep twenty people going for six weeks. There were two large tents, one for the family, one for my grandfather which doubled as a portable office. When I asked my father where the servants and forestry staff slept he looked surprised. 'Outside of course,' he said, 'a Burmese can sleep anywhere and anyway they'd prefer to sleep outside.'

Having decided which day the tour would begin, my grandfather would have the pack elephants brought up to the house the previous day. Every elephant had its own mahout, or *oozie*, as the minders were called in Burma, and every *oozie* had an assistant to walk beside the beast carrying a short spear for prodding it into obedience while the *oozie* rode aloft on its head. If the elephant was young or known to be bad-tempered there would be two assistants, one on each side. So up the drive to the house the four huge beasts would lumber, the tiny figures of the *oozies* sitting cross-legged on the top of their heads between the ears wielding long crops to give directions.

One elephant would carry a pannier consisting of two six-foot wooden boxes, like coffins, with hinged lids. These were for the cooking utensils and other household items. Another would have a similar sort of device, except that instead of hinged boxes there would be two six-foot-long wooden seats on either side of its swaying back filled with brightly coloured woven cushions and a sun canopy. This was where grandmother and the older children sat on the journey. A third elephant had two three-foot-high wicker panniers attached to its back. This was where the younger children would be placed, so that they could sleep or crawl about without danger of falling out. Clothes, linen and dried food were also stored here. The last elephant carried the tents and the other heavy equipment. This was always the biggest, strongest beast because the weight he had to bear was colossal. Eighty years ago tents were not the convenient light-weight constructions they are now. They were made of heavy canvas with numerous metal poles and ropes and it took a team of men several hours to erect them. There were also the chains which the *oozies* attached to the elephants' legs every night, not to tether them but to permit their minders to trace them in the morning. Pulling heavy chains prevented the animals from roaming too far afield and it was easy enough for the *oozies* and their assistants to track them down at first light and bring them back to the camp.

It isn't hard to imagine the frenzied activity that preceded every tour: the elephants kneeling passively while bundle after bundle was handed up and stowed, my grandfather standing on the steps in khaki shorts issuing orders. He alone of the assembly would be riding a horse, a relief horse following the procession, led by the groom. Only the family were provided with transport, everyone else walked behind, some carrying the more delicate items such as the Storm King oil lamps which might get broken on a constantly swaying elephant's back. How my father loved those expeditions. There was so much noise and colour and commotion. When they passed through a village everyone would come running out to see them, to sell them things or just to join in for a while, the children singing and dancing and clapping their hands. My grandmother would let the older children get down and join in, keeping a superior distance from the common crowd as befitted a *thakin ma gyi* (the big mistress).

It was when they passed through the Gurkha villages that they stocked up on provisions. The Gurkhas were famous for their smallholdings, their neatly planted crops. Every Gurkha household had its own milch cow and my father's cook would fill the billy cans and buy strawberries as a treat for supper. In amongst the cooking utensils were square glass jars fitted with a churning mechanism operated by a handle. She would half-fill these jars with the milk and give them to the children to churn as they sat swaying on top of the elephant. My father says he can still remember the fun of turning the handle round and round trying to be the first to make the butter.

No wonder my grandfather missed Burma so much when he retired. Those annual excursions up-country riding alongside the elephants, his beautiful wife and five happy children waving at him, his household staff carrying the Storm King lanterns, garlands of flowers, and baskets of tamarinds and mangoes, running and skipping behind.

He must have felt like a Saw Bwa himself or even a Mogul emperor marching at the head of his army.

At eleven or so the caravanserai would halt and pitch camp where they might stay for two or three days for the District Forest Officer to do a bit of work. My father, not just because he was the oldest boy but because he was genuinely interested, would go with his father and the other forest officers. Only two McHarg sons went into the business when they finished their education, my father and Jimmy, who has always been referred to as the black sheep of the family. My other uncles became desk-bound civil servants, Johnny in Customs and Excise, Peter joining the army before he emigrated to Australia. The purpose of these tours was to earmark the teak trees which were ready for felling. With an advance party of servants hacking a path for him, my grandfather, followed by young Maung Nyi, would reach the designated tree and measure its circumference. He didn't bother with a tape, he knew just by encircling its girth with his arms at chest height whether it had reached maturity. Then, having marked the tree, he would move on, leaving his men to prepare it.

This was the bit my father liked. The men would strip the bark from the roots up to eight feet all round the trunk to stop the sap rising, eventually killing it. The tree would be left thus for three years, all its natural moisture drying out so that when the loggers came and started the lengthy process of felling, the logs could be dragged by elephants to the nearest river, and would float downstream to the sawmills.

Every forestry worker had a tool called a hammer which was really a branding iron with his own identification number. (It was with one of these that Ma Nu's brother tried to kill the supervisor.) My father still remembers his number – SB 106, the initials representing Steel Brothers. When a tree was designated ready for felling the forestry officer who had selected it would stamp his number on to the trunk and again at the base of the tree. This practice ensured that every log reaching the saw mills had an identification tag. If the log turned out to be a dud, too green or partly rotten, the officer who had selected it could be called in for questioning. And since there would be a corresponding brand on the remaining tree stump a post-mortem could be carried out if necessary.

Both my parents and my stepfather, David James, have fascinating stories to tell about working in the teak forest with elephants. When my father was working with Steel Brothers, my mother used to accompany him on cold-season tours. It's the nearest thing I have to a family business. *Elephant Bill*, Billy Williams's classic account of his life working with the Bombay Burmah Trading Corporation captures the atmosphere. My stepfather knew Billy Williams and in the copy of *Elephant Bill* we had at North Lodge there's a photograph of my stepfather and the author supervising a felling at a logging camp.

The best stories were those told by the *oozies*. It goes without saying – just look at the size of them – that working with elephants can be dangerous. They are extremely sensitive animals with as many quirks and foibles as their masters. There were some, for instance, who would only allow you to approach them on the left. Try sneaking up on the right and you'd get a lash from that waving trunk. The most dangerous time was when the male elephants were on heat, or 'on must', as they called it, when they were likely to attack anyone approaching them. There was one legendary elephant whose story was always asked for on these family expeditions. I can see my father and his brothers and sisters sitting open-mouthed as the *oozie* tells it, their hands mechanically turning the handles of their butter churns.

This particular animal had somehow broken free from its tracking chains and run off to join a herd of wild elephants. Its *oozie* and a band of helpers tried to catch it without success. In the end they resorted to guile. They discovered the elephant's favourite feeding area and dug huge pits round it camouflaged with fallen branches. It sounds a bit like Winnie the Pooh's heffalump trap. Then they laid in wait and hoped the tusker would fall into a hole. It didn't. It used its trunk as a sort of mine detector, discovered the carefully arranged branches and casually placed camouflage palm leaves, hurled them in the air, skirted delicately round the hole and thundered off to join its wild companions. They tried another ploy. Someone had noticed that this particular animal was partial to tamarind leaves. (So incidentally, is my mother. She says there's nothing more delectable than a soup made of boiled tamarind leaves, as the perfect accompaniment to curry and rice.) The patient, if increasingly desperate, *oozie* collected a great quantity of tamarind leaves, sprinkled them with a generous dose of opium (most of the Burmese smoked the stuff in pipes after their evening meal) and once again lay in wait. This time it worked. The elephant ate the tamarind leaves and almost immediately the opium took effect. As it headed off towards the wild it staggered a little and stopped to lean heavily against the nearest tree. The *oozie* and his mates, armed with spears, came running out to catch it but, with a final desperate effort, the beast charged drunkenly off, faster than its pursuers could catch him. They tried the tamarind trick again but the canny old elephant knew the score and rejected it.

'So what happened in the end?' I asked my father when he told me the story, just as he must have asked the *oozie* telling him the story for the first time seventy years ago. I too told it to my four-year-old son at bedtime. Writing it down now is breaking one of those time-honoured legends passed down from generation to generation by word of mouth only.

In the end the *oozie* went to the wise man of the village and asked his advice. *Oozies* know all there is to know about elephants, that's why they're *oozies*, but maybe the wise man of this particular village was a retired *oozie*.

'What you must do', said the wise man, 'is tire the beast out. You must just chase him all day without a break so that he cannot stop to rest or to eat or drink and that way he will be so weary at nightfall you will be able to catch him and chain him up.'

So the *oozie* collected all the men and boys he could muster and placed them in strategic positions around the district where the rogue elephant was known to be. Armed with slings and spears the vanguard singled out their target, separated from the herd. 'This sounds difficult enough but it's easy if you know what you're doing,' my father said, and the Great Chase began. They chased the elephant towards a certain small hill and when they tired and dropped back, the second team of chasers on top of the hill chased the elephant down the other side and up another hill where a third team was waiting and so it went on and on all morning, all afternoon, all evening. The first team, rested and refreshed, came in for a second shift, as did their friends in the next team, but the poor elephant was never allowed a minute's rest. And yet he gave them the slip again. It was getting dark by now and for a while they thought they'd lost him.

And then someone heard a pitiful muffled roar. The canny old elephant had squeezed his great weary bulk through a narrow gulley along a dried-up river bed but unfortunately it wasn't dry enough. There was still a thick layer of dark sticky chocolate mud at the bottom and the elephant hadn't enough strength to drag its feet out. There it stood in the moonlight, like an enormous fly caught on a strip of fly paper, trumpeting feebly. Easy enough for the *oozie* to run down and attach the chains.

Travelling with elephants, however pleasant, for two months every year wasn't real life. Real life was living in Mogok and going to the local school where the lessons were in Burmese. It is now 1925 and my grandfather, aged sixty, is due for retirement. He has promised his mother in England – well this is the story he tells Ma Nu anyway – that he will die in his native land. The time has come to think about the future without him. What he wants most for his children is that they should be brought up in the English tradition. There are no English schools in Mogok, so a decision has to be made. The choice is between Moulmein and Maymyo. Both have English-speaking schools. 'Maymyo,' says Ma Nu without hesitation. It is practically next door.

My father says that the Government English High School in Maymyo has a very good reputation, the fees he remembers were £2 a month for five children. So WTT left his official residence in Mogok, took down the big ledger behind his desk for the last time, paid off the cooks, their assistants, the bearer, the gardener, the sweeper, the verandah *derzi* and the *syce*, and travelled up to Maymyo where he bought the family their own house. It wasn't as grand as the one allotted to the District Forest Officer and not nearly as commodious as the residence he'd had as Assistant Conservator of Forests without that unofficial coloured tribe in tow, but it was nice enough, in the wealthier part of town, and close to the GEHS.

There was one small set-back. Having taken a preliminary entrance test, it was discovered that the McHarg children were at least two years behind their peer group academically. To catch up the boys spent an embarrassing year at St Michael's Girls' Protestant School where my Auntie May stayed till she finished her education, while the boys went on to become little Templars, Argonauts and Adventurers. There were no English children at GEHS. Why would there be? There were precious few English wives and those who did stay out with their husbands sent the children back to England to school. Ninety per cent of the pupils were Anglo-Burmese. Pure Burmese were taught by the *phongyis* in the monasteries. The exceptions were children like the sons of the Saw Bwa.

When I asked if the Saw Bwa would have liked any of his daughters to marry Englishmen, my father looked at me blankly and said, 'Why not?' It's extraordinary – I have two parents whose perception of their Anglo-Burmese status couldn't be more different. My father doesn't appear to notice that he's foreign looking, sounding and thinking. These finer nuances of colour are lost on him. When I insist on thrusting them under his nose he simply cannot fathom what I'm talking about. My mother thinks of practically nothing else and, loath as I am to admit it, neither I suspect do I. 'But tell me,' I say for what seems the umpteenth time in the intermittent question-and-answer down-memory-lane sessions we've been having ever since I decided to track down my roots, 'are you saying that there wasn't any of the social class consciousness that there is in this country? You weren't better or worse because you were pure Burmese, pure English, Anglo-Burmese, Anglo-Indian, half Burmese, half Indian? It didn't make any difference?'

My father thinks about it. 'No,' he says, 'why should it?'

Here they are, then, the McHarg family in their new house in Maymyo, the children settled into their new schools not taking much notice, as is the way of children absorbed in their own affairs, of what their parents are up to, making provision for the family's future without its master. How much money WTT left his Burmese family I don't know. By English standards the cost of living in Burma in those days must have been ridiculously cheap. The Burmese were suspicious of banks so it's unlikely he would have left Ma Nu a savings account. An armful of gold bangles, bearing in mind that Burmese gold was twenty-four carat, was the equivalent to a handsome pension. But it isn't the humdrum running expenses that I'm interested in learning about when my father talks about the family moving to Maymyo.

I long to know what Ma Nu felt about the father of her five children leaving her for ever. Did she try and change his mind? Did she beg him to stay? Did she weep, plead, rage, call him heartless, cruel, treacherous? Did she threaten to kill herself, kill him, the children, write to his mother, blackmail his wife? In short did she do all the things that I would have done if my husband said he was walking out on me? No she didn't. She didn't even go to the station to see him off. Only May, Morny and Jimmy drove down to Maymyo station with their father and his cases the morning William Thomas Townley, Senior District Forest Officer for the Katha district of Upper Burma, went home to England. I have lost count of how many times I have asked my father to tell me about that day. He seems surprised at my curiosity. He doesn't seem to understand, as I am willing him to understand, that this was the most momentous, the most important, the saddest day of his young life.

Picture it yourself, my tall, slim grandmother not yet thirty-five, still beautiful, my dignified white-headed, albeit short, grandfather (he improved with age if the camera isn't lying). They didn't promise to write, how could they? Ma Nu's English, even after fifteen years of living with my grandfather, was elementary. She could understand it but she couldn't speak it and she definitely couldn't read it. My grandfather spoke Burmese but couldn't write it, so how would letters have helped unless a translator was at hand? After their last night together my grandfather would be busy packing and Ma Nu would go about her daily business, then the tonga would arrive and she might call out, 'Come children, come quickly and say goodbye to your father.' And out they all come running, the boys from playing football perhaps on the *maidan* in front of the Gymkhana Club. May, fifteen, small and studious – she hasn't inherited her mother's height – is inside, studying in her room. If they had been warned of this parting (my father says he doesn't remember any warning) they haven't taken it in. Their father has gone away on trips without them before. This one doesn't seem much different.

So he shakes the boys by the hand and tells them to be good and gives May a hug, and then as he's getting into the seat behind the driver, who's already whipping up the horse, he suddenly turns round and says, 'Come on you older ones, Morny, Johnny, May, come and see me off at the station.' And because they love riding in the tonga, they jump in laughing and the little ones, Peter and Jimmy, beg to come too but Ma Nu says, 'Hush, you're too small, stay with me.' And at last the tonga drives away, William waving his hat and looking back for a last time at his boys, their mother. Who knows? Perhaps he was trying to take it all in, the entire domestic scene, house, garden, family, servants, the complete colonial life-style into which he had thrown himself, inextricably attached himself, for the last fifteen years and which in half an hour would be gone for ever.

I don't know, and since I shall never know what was going through my grandfather's mind at that stage, let us continue on that last tonga ride to Maymyo station where they can hear the train already at the platform as they turn the corner. It is a steam train, of course, making all those delightful noises given to steam trains. The boys are enchanted, even May cannot hide her pleasure at being part of such an exciting excursion. The driver hands down the cases, a porter carries them to my grandfather's first-class reserved wood-panelled compartment in which he will travel all the way to Rangoon via Mandalay and Thazi. He shows them all the interesting little gadgets that a first-class private compartment offers: the light switches, the bell to call the attendant, the place to set your whisky glass. And then the whistle calls. 'Quick now children, hurry, hurry, you don't want to be left aboard and have to jump out. Off you go.' And they go. They stand, three small figures on the platform, waving and waving. Slowly gathering speed, the train chugs out of the station. My grandfather has opened the window as wide as it will go and he leans out now waving a big, clean, white handkerchief. It is all very noisy, other people are waving but they can see the white handkerchief fluttering and then they can see their father leaning out as far as he dares, the entire upper half of his body straining out of the window to allow the old man with white hair a last long glimpse of those three tiny figures. The track is straight for half a mile or so and then it turns a wide sweep to the left and suddenly the handkerchief, the white hair, the train have disappeared.

'We'd better go home,' says May.

4 ∫

Charlie Lloyd's Daughter

And now to my mother whose family cupboards hold no skeletons but whose confused feelings about her dual nationality must be the root cause of my own inhibitions. I don't know much about my maternal grandfather, Charlie Lloyd. No one does.

'Promise me you'll find out about Charlie,' my mother says. 'I'd like to know more about him. His cousin, Sir Idris Lloyd, was a big noise in the government you know.' You cannot do better in my mother's eyes than be a big noise. And then she gives me various birth date alternatives – 'It was either 5 September 1865 or 11 November 1856' – which I'm supposed to take round to St Catherine's House. Minutes later (this is what my mother thinks) the attendant comes back and hands me a sheet of vellum printed with a sort or *Who's Who* entry on the following lines:

LLOYD, Charles Ernest born 5 September 1865 or 11 November 1856, extremely well connected, public-school educated, handsome, athletic. Big Noise. m. Ma Shweh Ohn with royal connections from Bassein, Union of

Burma, one d. Marjorie b. 1914. Rec. polo. Clubs: Gymkhana, Taunggyi.

When I said my mother was a racist I was underselling her. My mother sees everything in terms of skin tone. Ask her about her school friends, boy-friends, even her own family and the first thing she will tell you is what colour they are. The Anglo-Burmese come in a variety of colourways from ivory to coffee, darker if, as my mother says, they have dog-Indian blood. My mother is pale, a couple of shades off ivory, my father is nearer Gold Blend. I'm somewhere in the middle and though my children look vaguely foreign it has nothing to do with skin tone.

At the beginning of this book I said that all I wanted was to be English. I could have added that all my mother wanted was to be white. The next-best thing to being white yourself was to marry someone who was. To this day I cannot imagine how she came to marry my father. She would have been better off with his younger brother Johnny who is unnervingly pale for an Anglo-Burmese, almost albino. She says by way of explanation that she married McHarg on the rebound. She was actually in love with an RAF pilot she had met when they were both acting in a production of *The Importance of Being Earnest* for an amateur dramatic society in Rangoon. She isn't forthcoming as to why the relationship ended. Maybe the pilot had qualms about going native. Or maybe it was his mother back in Blighty who wrote to tell him about her own qualms.

When I was engaged for the first time, a long-standing friend of my fiancé's family warned him against marrying me because of how the children might turn out. 'How might the children turn out?' asked my fiancé, genuinely mystified. 'Well you never know, there might be a throw-back.

They could be black,' said the friend. It's the sort of remark my mother might have made.

So Biggles didn't tie the knot and she ended up not only wedded to my father but doing the proposing as well. She was twenty-six. Most of her friends were married and she saw the shelf looming. Besides, as I've already said, my father was an outstandingly handsome man. If it hadn't been for the war it probably wouldn't have lasted very long. They hardly saw each other. My father was called up, my mother and older sister, aged three, trekked overland to India where she joined the WACI (Women's Army Corps India), acquired a sexy uniform, and spent her war years having a fling with British officers. My father, on unexpected home leave, had a fight with one of her suitors, a major in the Coldstream Guards, on a railway station in Mysore. By the time they got to England it was inevitable they would split up as soon as my mother had found a white man. She did, as fate would have it, in the jungles of Borneo.

'What on earth would have happened to us if I hadn't met David,' my mother is wont to say. She invariably says it when I have just returned from a visit to my father in Kenton. 'Suburbia,' says my mother, as if she were saying athlete's foot. 'Ugh how I hated suburbia, all those net curtains.'

This is unfair when you remember how smug we felt with our bay windows and net curtains at 34 Christchurch and how invincible when we had moved to our state-of-the-art Tudor gabled semi on Woodcock Hill.

'You'd never have got anywhere if we had stayed in Kenton with Daddy. You wouldn't have gone to university of course. You'd have been ashamed to bring your friends home. We owe everything to Dweedle.'

My poor long-suffering stepfather. His name was David James. He was Welsh. David in Welsh is Dewi, which became Dwe on the tongues of his two small stepdaughters. My mother, ever sentimental, called him Dweedle. Poor David. Some people called him Dwiddle.

All my mother's complexes come from growing up Anglo-Burmese in a society which regarded half-castes as misfits. Blame the Raj. It was all very well for William Thomas Townley McHarg and Charles Ernest Lloyd to take up with native women. To be sure they were regarded as eccentric, but when the time came for them to return home alone, leaving their native excesses behind them, what difference did it make?

If my mother's complex comes from being touched with the tar brush – as the English so endearingly put it – how come my father isn't as obsessed with skin tone and social status? It's quite simple – he is neither imaginative nor ambitious. Ask him if he would prefer to have been British instead of Anglo and he would look at you oddly and say, 'But how could I be British, Susan, when my mother was a Shan?'

'Yes, yes, Daddy we know all that, all we're saying is, would you have wanted it to be different, can you imagine it being different?' No of course he couldn't. Sitting there on that incongruous *chaise longue* in his socks he's not prepared to imagine anything.

'Typical bloody Burman. All they want to do is sit under a mango tree and smoke cheroots. No ambition at all,' says my mother who from the start had ambitions and aspirations. 'My mother always said, "Marjorie, you are not of us, you are European, you will go away and live a different life to us."' And because she was so much lighter than her cousins, who taunted her for being a whitey, she thought of herself as English and despised anyone with darker skin, whether Burmese, Anglo or dog-Indian. The fact that the pure Burmese despised the Anglos as heartily didn't occur to her. *Ka bia*, half and half, was the Burmese equivalent of *kway Kalas*. Did either of my grandfathers, or any of the thousands of other British colonials who took up with the natives, imagine how their mixed-race children would fare?

My father's sanguine attitude could be the result of the stability and security that his father gave to the family, even when he had left Burma. He kept in touch, he sent cheques, he cared about them. My mother on the other hand hardly knew her father. He died when she was three. If she were to spend half an hour with a shrink I bet he'd tell her that all her ambitions to rise above her native background and to marry a white man are based on her feelings for her father. He sounds interesting. Maybe I should go to St Catherine's House and find out more, but what would a few facts about his place of birth and the parish in which he'd been baptised tell me about his character? What I know of him is sketchy. It has to be. It comes from my mother who got it from her mother who only knew Charlie for four years.

When my grandfather, Charlie Lloyd, married my grandmother he was fifty-six, she was seventeen. I say 'married' because, even though the Burmese in those days had no official marriage ceremony, Charlie was a bachelor. This, as far as anyone knew, was his first stab at a permanent relationship. Up to the time he met my grandmother he had led a typical colonial bachelor's life. He was in the Imperial Police, same as George Orwell. When he got married in Taunggyi he was Chief of Police for the region, definitely a big noise, if not quite as exalted as his cousin Sir Idris in Rangoon. His chief passions beside his work were polo and whisky. He was a brilliant polo player, keeping two strings of ponies and when the Prince of Wales visited Burma he was invited to join the royal team. He had scores of silver polo cups and a servant whose only duty was to polish them. His large government residence close to the river was staffed with twenty servants. He had six government launches permanently moored on the river – one for his own personal use, one for his staff, one for his polo ponies, one for his trophies and one for ice. That makes five, I said. My mother doesn't remember what the sixth launch contained. I reckon it was whisky. Charlie never drank water. He said it was the surest route to cholera. Two fingers of rye, he declared, were the best protection against native diseases.

If Charlie Lloyd hadn't died of drink, would he, I wonder, have taken my grandmother home to Wales when he retired? He wanted her to go on leave with him and meet his mother soon after they met. My grandmother, who wasn't a traveller, said she would sail with him as far as Colombo in what was then Ceylon. She wanted to make a pilgrimage to the temple where the holy relic of the Lord Buddha's tooth was enshrined. Like most Burmese women, she was very religious. Any spare money she had went to the monastery. Years later, when my mother was settled in Hampshire with my stepfather, my grandmother became ill. My mother wanted to visit her but was refused an entry visa to Burma. She was classified as unpatriotic for leaving the country during the war. She wrote to Grannie saying she would send her an air ticket to come and live with us in England. My grandmother refused. An aeroplane would have to fly over her pagoda – a good Buddhist would never place himself above the Lord Buddha.

When I went to Burma for the first time I bought a small carved wooden statue of Buddha from a stall in the Maha Muni Pagoda. My niece studying mathematics at Mandalay University said, 'Please, Auntie, take care to set your Lord Buddha higher than anything else in the room. It is not good for Him to be low.'

So Grannie only went as far as Colombo and Charlie sailed on home. I want to picture her travelling but I cannot. She surely didn't carry a suitcase, *longyi* and suitcases don't go together. Maybe all her needs could be packed into a Shan bag. As for money, apart from loose change, she would be wearing it in the form of jewellery. Charlie lavished his wife with jewellery. The first time he took her to Rangoon they went to P. Orr and Sons, the biggest jewellers in Burma. He said she could choose anything she wanted. My grandmother said she needed a watch. 'Show the lady your watches,' says Charlie and my grandmother chooses the smallest, thinking it will be the cheapest. Of course it isn't. It is the most expensive but Charlie just laughs and takes out his wallet.

My grandmother's name was Ma Shweh Ohn which means Miss Field of Gold and when she married she became Daw Shweh Ohn (*Daw* means Mrs), but Charlie always called her Fatty. This must have been a private joke because she was tiny, less than five foot, fragile as a flower, with a whittled waist. She came originally from Bassein, the delta region the other side of the country from Taunggyi but her parents had moved north taking their two daughters with them. The Burmese have small families, rarely more than two children which makes naming them simple. Most families have a Ko Ko, which means big brother or a Nyi Nyi which means little brother. My grandmother's older sister Daw Sein would have been called Ma Ma Gyi, meaning big sister, while she would have been Ma Ma Lay, little sister. Their formal names were used mainly for official documents. The Anglo-Burmese following Victorian tradition went in for larger families and the usual stock of names popular at that time – George, Harold, Dennis, Marjorie, Winnie, Ethel.

Charlie adored the Burmese. 'He absolutely adored us,' says my mother, her voice shaking with emotion. She has temporarily forgotten that she is not of them, that she is destined to rise above them and marry a white man. 'In those days of the Raj the British were really looked up to,

they really were and the Anglo-Burmese shared some of
this respect. They weren't like the Anglo-Indians who were
treated like dirt. We Burmese were considered special. It
was because of our temperament. The Burman feels no
one to be his equal, no not even the British. The only
race we consider to be more intelligent than us are the
Chinese.'

Of course Charlie must have liked the Burmese, I say,
because he chose to live there and, what's more, marry
one. My mother who has just remembered that her father's
sister, another May, was married to a General Prendergast,
which will make it easier for me to check him out when
I get to St Catherine's House, replies that no it wasn't just
his wife he adored, it was all the Burmese and their way
of life. When he invited other expatriates to his residence
he did not, as William Thomas Townley had done, merely
introduce his wife and then pass on into his own quarters
for a formal meal. He made his British guests sit cross-legged
on the floor and eat curry – even the Anglican bishop in his
cassock.

Then there was the man newly arrived from England
who made derogatory remarks about the natives and their
primitive ways. My mother said I mustn't repeat this but it
was actually George Orwell.

'Don't be daft,' I said, 'George Orwell wasn't a racist. He
liked the Burmese.'

'Well then,' said my mother, not at all dismayed, 'it was
a friend of George Orwell's.' Even this seems unlikely. My
grandfather, annoyed by the racist remarks whoever they
were made by, persuaded the prettiest girls in Taunggyi to
parade up and down outside the bounder's house, dressed
in their prettiest *longyis*, carrying parasols. They must have
looked like a chorus line from *The Mikado*. Maybe that's
how he met my grandmother. Now there's a thought.

I've only seen one photograph of Charlie Lloyd, looking

darkly handsome in his police chief's uniform with a white sash. He is tall with a stiff military bearing, a monocle and a pasty complexion which may be the quality of the photograph, but is more likely to be the whisky. Those two fingers of rye took their toll. When he was dying he took Fatty's small hand in his and whispered that he was sorry, he wished he had done more for her and little Marjorie. He had done enough. Materially he had left his family extremely well off – by Burmese standards anyway. My mother remembers boxes of gold sovereigns and jewellery. Burmese women set great store by jewellery. My mother can remember every stone of every ear-ring she ever possessed. There are various superstitions associated with rubies, the Burmese national stone. It is, for instance, bad luck ever to suggest that a ruby is not worth the price the seller asks. The correct reply is to say: 'The ruby is very beautiful but I cannot afford it.' Diamonds, emeralds, sapphires, haggle for them all you like, but never for a ruby. When my grandmother needed cash she either used sovereigns or bartered one of the dozens of gold bangles Charlie was always giving her.

Charlie Lloyd had a magnificent official funeral, worthy of his rank, with all the big noises up from Rangoon parading past his coffin and a military band. Not, however, his favourite bagpipes. When my grandmother was in labour giving birth to my mother Charlie despatched his Gurkha orderly to march up and down in front of the window playing the bagpipes to drown out the noise. My mother claims to have heard the music in the womb and has hated the bagpipes ever since. Beside him in his coffin Daw Shweh Ohn placed three of her husband's polo trophies, two tins of his favourite Camel cigarettes and his razor so that he would look decent when he got to the other world. The rest of his trophies she packed up and sent to his mother in Wales. She was a widow, just twenty-one, with a baby daughter and her only sister living a day's journey away in Mandalay. Since my mother never mentions her grandparents it is safe to assume they were both dead at this time.

Now for the royal connection. My great-grandmother, Ma Shweh Ohn's mother, was a lady-in-waiting to Queen Supayalat, the last Queen of Burma. When their majesties were invited to abdicate in favour of the Raj, and did so with perfect propriety and no bloodshed, my great-grandmother, so the story goes, escaped from the royal palace in Mandalay by swimming across the moat.

'But if it was a bloodless coup why did she have to escape?' I asked my mother.

'Because she was stealing a large gold ceremonial jar which she hid under her *longyi* when she swam to safety.'

I'm not sure what to make of this story. It doesn't stand up to close scrutiny. For a start my mother only told me about this exciting royal connection when she was well into her seventies. The older she gets the more she leans towards her Burmese origins. I quite often hear her telling strangers, visiting gas repair men and so on, about her childhood, her sentences beginning 'We Burmese . . .' She'd never have said that when she married my stepfather and settled down to a new genteel life in the Home Counties. On the other hand she might, as old people do, suddenly recall something that had lain forgotten in her memory for more than half a century. My main reason to suspect the truth of the story of the ceremonial jar is that oriental women are not by nature athletic. They aren't the right shape. The idea of one of these frail creatures stuffing a jar under her skirt and then free-styling across the palace moat seems unlikely. 'What happened to the jar?' I asked. My mother doesn't know. She said it was a *lepet* jar, *lepet* being a delicacy made from ginger and green tea, pickled with sesame seeds, garlic and oil. It is very pungent, cut into small cubes and nibbled, as you would a Twiglet. An invitation to a royal event would be accompanied by a small piece of *lepet* wrapped in a leaf like a samosa and fastened with a clove.

I wish my mother could remember more about Charlie Lloyd, but why would she? I was three when we left Burma and I remember nothing about it. She has two lasting memories of her father. The first is of him scratching the soles of her tiny baby shoes so that she wouldn't slip. I was surprised at this one. I didn't think Burmese children wore shoes and, even if they did, how could one slip on a mud floor? My mother was shocked. 'We had a very beautiful residence with polished parquet floors. Of course I might have slipped.' The second memory she has is of crawling over his coffin to look at his face. I wonder what the Chief of Police would have made of this, not a lot I dare say. He wanted his daughter to be educated in the English way which doesn't include small children crawling over coffins.

A year after Charlie died my mother aged four was sent away to a baptist missionary school called St Matthew's in Moulmein way down on the Tenasserim Peninsula. It took two days to get there by train. Miss Fairclough, the headmistress encouraged the children to call her Mummy. Since the pupils went home for only one month in the year, she really was their surrogate mother. They wore proper English school uniform, brown gym-slips, cream blouses and knee socks.

When my grandmother first left my mother at St Matthew's she brought warm clothing imagining it would get as cold in winter as it did in the Upper Shan States. The other children sniggered at my mother's trunk full of thick jerseys and coats. A week after she arrived at St Matthew's she ran away. Not far. She was taken in by a baptist missionary family who later asked if they could adopt her. My grandmother declined the offer.

The idea of sending a four-year-old away to school for

eleven months of the year sounds heartless. My grand-mother had only been widowed a year. Surely she would have wanted to keep little Marjorie with her for company? 'She did it because she wanted the best for me,' says my mother. And the best was a school where the children spoke English, sang hymns, did two Shakespeare plays a term and read Dryden and poems from the *Oxford Book of English Verse*. I wonder if my grandmother really thought like that or whether she was just doing as she knew her husband would have wanted. Compared with my other grandmother, Ma Nu, who bribed her sons with bicycles into going through with the *shin-pyu* ceremony in direct opposition to her husband's wishes, Daw Shweh Ohn sounds far more docile.

After a couple of years at St Matthew's my mother practically forgot how to speak Burmese which further estranged her from her mother. She says she remembers going home for that one month in the year and actually hiding from this strange little woman in the *longyi* with jasmine in her hair and the cheroot in her hand, so different from Mummy Fairclough back in Moulmein. I felt the same when, after leaving me in a Hertfordshire convent for two years to join my father in Borneo, my mother arrived to collect me. Two years in Borneo under the Sarawak sun had done for whitey, she looked to my eight-year-old eyes like something from the African jungle, and I hid behind Reverend Mother's black skirts begging her not to let this woman take me away.

My mother can recall plenty about her school, where before meals the younger girls did crow duty to keep the birds off the tables (they ate in the open), and she and her best friend Dolly Corrie made a pact that they would never be friends with ugly girls or girls with dark skins. Beastly little prigs. Miss Fairclough ran St Matthew's Girls' School on Cheltenham Ladies College principles. At Christmas the girls sang 'In the Bleak Mid-Winter', and wondered what snow could look like. All the pupils except Dolly Corrie were Anglo-Burmese, the daughters of British fathers working for British forestry or mining companies or the civil service. Dolly Corrie's parents were both English, he was a river pilot for the Irrawaddy Flotilla Company and had seven children all educated in mission schools. The children played English games, hockey and netball and lacrosse and at break they played five stones. My mother's five-stones partner was a girl called Nancy Wemyss, light-skinned of course, whose father worked for a mining company. Nancy's five stones were five rubies. She swapped them for my mother's most precious possession, a matchbox filled with cotton wool.

How I loathe that matchbox. It is my mother's touchstone to measure how wonderful her childhood values were and how appalling my children's values are. Here's how it works. My mother hears two of my children fighting over a plastic racing car. 'When I was their age', she says, 'I didn't have any of those expensive toys. All I had was a little piece of cotton wool in a matchbox, and it was all I wanted. I played with it for hours.' And her mouth starts to tremble. Or else a child has left a bicycle out in the rain. My mother's mouth puckers into a small dried olive. 'Children these days have no respect for anything. They don't look after anything. When I think how I treasured my little piece of cotton wool in a matchbox.' For all its modesty my mother's matchbox must have had some clout or why would Nancy Wemyss have swapped her five-stone rubies for it?

Poor Miss Fairclough. She may have aspired to being the Cheltenham Ladies College of the East but there were aspects of St Matthew's that simply didn't fit the mould. Crow duty for instance. And the lavatories, which my mother recalls with a shudder. There was no plumbing. In an outbuilding stood a row of Ali Baba clay jars on which the children would squat. The jars were half filled with water which attracted snakes. It was not uncommon for a girl sitting on the jar to feel something slither up beside her. My mother left St Matthew's with honours in most school certificate subjects, a life-long terror of snakes and constipation.

In the month they were reunited my grandmother liked to show off her so very English child and took her to visit her friends every afternoon. The Burmese ladies would sit cross-legged on the floor gossiping, sipping tea, eating gram crackers and *lepet*, while my mother in smocked party frock with puffed sleeves sat on a stool bored stiff, not understanding a word that was being said. Sometimes my grandmother would look up and ask her to recite something she had learned at school, so little Marjorie would get off her stool, pull up her white socks and intone a few lines from *Paradise Lost*. Afterwards the ladies would pat her head and give her a few *pyas* as a reward.

Impressing her friends with her clever daughter's party tricks was only half the story. My grandmother may have handed over her daughter's education to English missionaries but she could still have a small influence. When my mother was tucked up for the night under her mosquito net my grandmother would get in beside her and tell her the history of Burma, wonderful stories about Kings and Queens and heroic battles with the enemies from Siam and folk legends and religious tales about the Lord Buddha. As she talked she would stab at intruding mosquitoes with the end of her cheroot, burning holes in the mosquito net as she did so, and my mother would fall asleep counting the holes, her imagination fired by the adventures she had just heard.

'Tell me about the Burmese Kings and Queens,' I asked, but my mother said she had forgotten them all.

My mother's memories of her childhood are patchy. The information has to trickle out in its own time or be nudged into her memory by association. If, for instance, she sees me washing a child's hair she at once remembers how her mother washed her hair in Taunggyi with the bark of the Shore tree, boiling pieces with lemon and tamarind rind and all sorts of spices to produce a magnificent lather which left your hair squeaking. And then once a month my grandmother would pour coconut oil over her hair to keep it glossy and supple. I brought home a jar from Burma to do the same to mine but it solidified in the cold climate and looked like lard. Or if I'm sewing a button on to my son's blazer as he dashes out of the door to get to school on time my mother will say, Cassandra-like, that it is unlucky to sew anything on to a living person because only the dead are sewn into their shrouds. Same with sewing a cushion or a pillowcase, you always leave a gap to allow the evil spirit to escape. There is a Burmese superstition to suit every occasion. Half the time I think my mother just makes them up on the spur of the moment.

When my mother was fourteen my grandmother remarried. Enter the famous Ko Ko, onion, tobacco and lacquer broker. They had two children, Betty and Neil, and fluctuated between extreme wealth and extreme poverty according to Ko Ko's deals. Sometimes they were so poor that my grandmother would have to sell a favourite piece of jewellery to buy her daughter's train ticket to school. 'But this was because she insisted on buying me a first-class ticket. That was always the way in our family. Keeping up appearances.' At some point the household expanded further to take in my grandmother's elder sister's two children. May and Jimmy were a little older than my mother who held a lone Anglo place between her full Burmese cousins and step-siblings. So I have an Auntie May on both sides of the family which is confusing, but I blame the popularity of Princess May of Teck who had become Queen Mary on the accession of George V.

When they were rich they had servants. It was from the verandah *derzi* that my mother learned how to sew. Ko Ko went up country to the Chinese border where the villagers were so poor they would willingly sell a child for a bag of salt or a bag of sugar, and bought two young girls who helped my grandmother in the house. They did all the heavy work but they were treated as members of the family. If Ko Ko bought a present for his own children, he would automatically buy presents for the adopted ones as well.

My mother's half-sister Betty was spared the rigours of St Matthew's. Not only was she wholly Burmese but, according to my mother, who as we now know is the recognised expert in these matters, was very, very dark indeed. 'I think Ko Ko had some Indian in him, Betty looked sort of Indian,' she said.

My mother wanted to be a doctor and study at Rangoon University. By this time Ko Ko had lost all his money, all the *stik lak* in his go-down had turned to dust and he was on his uppers. Seven years in medical school was out of the question and Marjorie Lloyd followed Auntie May to teachers' training college instead. She joined the Rangoon amateur dramatic society. This was in the early 'thirties when Rangoon was one of the most fashionable centres in the Orient. I read somewhere that in 1930 Rangoon airport was the busiest in South-East Asia. Academics aspired to getting a job at the university and its academic standards were considered to be higher than anything outside the UK.

The Chancellor, Professor Eggar, ran it on Oxbridge lines. Every summer they held an ersatz Henley Regatta, complete with blazers, boaters, Pimm's on the lawn and all the usual sculling races on the Inya Lake. What, I wonder, did all those imported academics make of the students promenading in their striped blazers? I have this picture of all the pukka Brits standing on one side sniggering and making snide remarks about coconut Marys.

The story goes that, ever since they started holding the regatta, when the boats reached a particular point in the lake during the diamond sculls race they always capsized. Year after year it happened with no good reason and then someone suggested to the Chancellor that it was the *nyats*. *Nyats*, what *nyats*? I can hear him reply irritably. Politely, the Burmese would explain how the spirits of the lake might be offended by all the annual revelry which was why they were capsizing the boats. Tommy-rot, he probably said and dined out on the story for the next year and then it was regatta time again and the diamond sculls and, whoops, over went the boats once more. Would it have been the Chancellor or one of his minions who eventually asked the Burmese who first mentioned the possibility of *nyat* interference, how they might solve the problem? The *nyats* had to be propitiated, was the answer. They had to be offered gifts and prayers and maybe that way they would forgive. So come the next regatta, before the first Pimm's was drunk or the first race started a boat full of *phongyis* rowed to the trouble spot in the lake. The *phongyis* chanted prayers, threw gifts of fruit and garlands of flowers into the water, sang songs, and then rowed back to shore. When it was time for the diamond sculls everyone waited expectantly. The starting gun fired, the boats neared the point of no return and this time carried on without interruption. Everyone cheered. The Brits in the corner were momentarily nonplussed but recovered, to make even snider and wittier remarks about the extraordinary beliefs and customs of the Burmese, but every regatta thereafter before the first Pimm's was drunk, the boat full of *phongyis*, papayas and mangoes would set out to propitiate the *nyats*.

My mother married Morny McHarg on 1 April 1940. She says she had cold feet about it the day before and told her mother she wanted to call it off. My grandmother, a widow for the second time by now – Ko Ko had died of cholera the year before – said they would suffer serious loss of face if there were no wedding. How could they put people off at this late stage without looking ridiculous? Poor Grannie, when Ko Ko died, penniless as usual, she found some IOUs among his things and tried to redeem them. One man said he would pay her in kind. Next day she heard chains clanking outside the house – she had been sent an elephant.

My father was already working for Steel Brothers, thanks to a contact of William Thomas Townley's, and, though my mother strenuously denies it now, I think they were happy enough. When I told her about my father's description of travelling with elephants up-country she said yes she knew all about that, she had done it often enough herself with McHarg and then she shut up quickly. She doesn't want to remember pleasant associations with him. It must be guilt. She changes the subject to the times she went into the jungle with Dwe, my stepfather, how all the Brits wore dinner-jackets and had baths in tin tubs with hot water provided by scores of servants.

I can't get to the bottom of this. She was still married to my father when she went out to Borneo. That's why she went, to join him and try to iron out their differences. David James was head of my father's section. How could the admittedly beautiful, but nevertheless *ka bia*, wife of one of his subordinates be carrying on with the big white chief in the jungle in front of all those servants? My mother was more likely looking on from the sidelines of my father's tent. I'm pretty sure *he* never wore a dinner-jacket.

My sister Jennifer was born in September 1941 into a more than comfortable home with servants. Pearl Harbor changed everything. My father was called up; my mother and the other Anglo-Burmese wives married to the employees of British companies were advised to head for India and safety. The only way out was to walk north from Mingun and reach India via the tea gardens of Assam.

To start with it all sounds like a bit of a party. Knowing that their home in Prome would soon be occupied by the advancing Japanese, my parents invited all their friends round, tipped every bottle of alcohol in the house into a huge vat and ladled out the Pearl Harbor cocktail. Their house was used as a staging post for people coming up from Rangoon on the way north to Mingun.

My uncle Peter and his wife Chico were among them. Another chance for my mother to slip in a skin-tone anecdote. 'Peter was a very presentable young man. He was very fair, Peter, as fair as your children and good-looking. He was an absolute little upstart anyway, but he was light. And I said to this fellow Gibson who worked for Steel Brothers, a bit of a big noise there, I said, "But why is Peter marrying Chico? She's so small and wizened and dark and tiny, he could have had anyone." And do you know what Gibson said to me? "Ssh Marjorie, her mother makes very good pickles."' My mother laughs throatily, she's a forty-a-day smoker and her laugh is so infectious you have to join in.

My mother wrote to Grannie that she was being evacuated with the baby and my grandmother drove to see her off from Mawchi, where Ko Ko had been working for a mining company before he died. 'Why don't you come too?' my mother suggested, and Grannie decided she would, provided my mother could wait for her to go home to fetch her jewels. But on the way back the car was commandeered by the army who gave her a horse instead. Never having ridden a horse in her life before, my grandmother made her way home to Mawchi as best she could and gave up ideas of escape, which is how we find her later dangling her valuables in the Inle Lake and being championed by the Saw Bwa.

Meanwhile my parents' house in Prome was chock-a-block with evacuees and eventually my mother too took the paddle steamer up to Mandalay. They had been warned not to take valuables on the trip because the route was stiff with dacoits. My mother seems to have had some kind of mental lapse. She was so busy packing her horse, groom, cook, cook's mate, *amah* and the baby on to the boat she forgot to pack any clothes. All she took with her was a bag of remnants left by the verandah *derzi*, which she later embroidered into a patchwork quilt.

All her wedding presents, silver and china she abandoned. It was an overnight journey to Mandalay with one stop at the mining town of Yenangyaung where my mother's life-long friend and would-be suitor came to say goodbye. His name was U Pe Kin. He too was Anglo-Burmese with some Indian blood. He was a Moslem and later, after the assassination of the entire Burmese Cabinet under Aung San in 1947, he left mining and worked for the Government. He went on to be Burmese ambassador in Moscow, Cairo and finally to the UN.

The boat trip sounds more like a party than an evacuation. They all had cabins. Coming down from the bar to hers my mother opened the wrong door and surprised an army chaplain kneeling down beside his bunk saying his prayers with a long cigar in his mouth. The boat was packed. The easiest means of travel in Burma in those days was by river. Those evacuees who couldn't get cabins would have had to sit on deck in the open, surrounded by poor families cooking over charcoal stoves and people selling fruit and cakes.

After Mandalay the refugees, as they were now being called, were transferred to the last staging post before the trek. Mingun is famous for having the largest civic bell ever struck and as they entered the town the bell was ringing.

'There was a chap called Atkinson in charge of refugees,' recalls my mother. 'And when he saw me, my horse, my groom, cook, cook's mate, *amah* and baby, he couldn't believe his eyes.'

'Where on earth do you think you're going?' he asked her (she was wearing jodhpurs and riding boots). 'On a picnic?' He commandeered the horse, the groom and the cook. 'You won't be needing a cook where you're going. There's no food,' he said cheerfully. But he let her keep the cook's mate, a twelve-year-old boy, and the nanny.

Both stayed with my mother in India through the war and came back with her to Burma afterwards. They enjoyed the same position with my parents as the two adopted girls had done in her mother's household. They became part of the family. Unlike the girls, they hadn't been swapped for a pound of salt and a pound of tea, they were paid wages. Once in the family, though, they would be treated like children, given clothes, even jewellery, and educated. 'They just became family,' says my mother.

The six-week trek into India began in mid-February 1942. There were thirty of them, mainly women and children with one or two men as protection. My sister was the only baby on the trek. She was five months old and because my mother was breast-feeding her she had been assigned a sedan chair carried by two bearers. After the first five days she gave up her sedan chair to an elderly woman with arthritis. With my mother was another woman who had been at St Matthew's, Margaret Hunley. When my mother stopped to feed the baby, Margaret stayed with her and they reminisced about school days. The target was twenty miles a day which didn't allow for many rest breaks. My mother developed a form of malaria called tertiary malaria which attacks every three days. She remembers feeling light-headed with fever but there was no question of stopping. At night they aimed to reach a camp set up for them in advance by the forestry workers where they could cook and sleep. But sometimes when the refugees reached these camps they found they had been burned down by dacoits, so they would have to sleep in the open. For the first few days they had rice and even a few vegetables but as they climbed into the mountains they had to rely on what they could get in the camps. Occasionally they came across independent travellers who would join their group. Everyone was frightened of dacoits. They were never attacked but they heard stories along the way about others not so lucky. Another of my mother's school friends who did the northern trek to India, more dangerous because the Japanese were nearer, tells how their group was attacked by Burmese bandits and actually rescued by a company of Japanese soldiers who gave them food.

Half-way through the trek there was an outbreak of typhoid. Everyone had to spend a week at a mountain staging camp to be inoculated. My tiny sister took the injection very badly and howled for days afterwards. She was very sick, covered in eczema and a rash the Burmese call St Anthony's fire, brought on by my mother's malaria. When she lifted her chin, the skin beneath it cracked. Margaret Hunley and my mother would pound their daily rice ration with stones to produce a coarse powder which they would rub on my sister's inflamed skin as if it were talcum powder. 'Poor little Jennifer, she was in a dreadful state, never stopped crying but it was all we could do for her,' says my mother, who cannot talk about the journey without weeping. She had a theory much later when my sister was diagnosed blind that the six weeks the baby spent being carried to India, constantly staring at the sun, had contributed to the condition. But this is not so. Retinitis pigmentosa is a hereditary disease.

Apart from the bundle of dressmaker's remnants my mother had brought only a dozen cotton nappies for my sister. Whenever they reached a camp she and Margaret would walk down to the stream and wash them. The water was always icy. Some of the more astute refugees had brought quantities of cigarettes with them which they sold to the others for one rupee each. Normally a tin of fifty cigarettes cost two rupees. My mother had no money to buy cigarettes. It was the longest period in her entire life she stopped smoking. She remembers a British forestry officer giving her a tin of cocoa at one of the camps. It was better than a lump of gold she said. The tea always tasted of chlorine. You might suppose the crystal-clear water flowing past the camps was pure until you saw a bloated body floating by.

The group didn't travel in a compact band. They straggled over half a mile or so, my mother, Margaret and the baby always at the back because my mother had to stop so often to feed Jenny. 'All right, Marjorie, see how quickly you can feed her this time. I'll keep a watch for tigers,' Margaret would say. They never saw a tiger but they were known to be around. Once they saw a young girl carrying a dead body over her shoulder. It was her father, they learned, but she refused to leave him because she had no spade to bury him. There were worse sights but my mother says that fortunately she had the capacity to block them from her memory.

Not at any time were they aware that there was a war going on around them. The only air-raid siren my mother ever heard was the night they left Mandalay to start the trek. It was the first and the last siren she heard because there were no air raids in India. As they approached the Indian border there were milestones along the trail saying 'Welcome to India'. Planes overhead dropped corned beef and cigarettes – manna from heaven especially the tins of Woodbines. My mother weighed four stone when she arrived in the tea gardens of Assam, her boots had string tied round the soles to keep them together. She had been in the same clothes, jodhpurs and a shirt, for six weeks. She admits it was her own fault that she didn't bring more things, food and clothing for herself. She wasn't thinking clearly in the turmoil of leaving. Other evacuees had brought dried food which kept them going but my mother has never been interested in food, either eating it or cooking it.

At Palel, the refugee camp the other side of the Indian border, the tea planters had set up sleeping and clothing tents for the new arrivals. 'Help yourself to as much as you want,' they were told. Women fought over fur coats and high-heeled sandals. My mother took only a shawl for Jenny, partly through pride and partly because she had never been given or bought a ready-made dress in her life. If she wanted a dress the *derzi* came over and sewed it on the verandah. One tea planter gave my mother a plate of bacon and eggs. She took it and burst into tears, she hadn't seen food like it since Prome.

From Palel the refugees were put in trains for Calcutta where they stayed in dormitories at the Loretto Convent. My mother had one contact in India, the former stage manager of *The Importance of Being Earnest*, the amateur theatricals in Rangoon where she had first met Biggles, her would-be fiancé. Denis O'Leary knew that she would be coming through to India at some stage along with the other company wives, so he checked with the nuns every day to see if her name was on the list. My mother says the Indians treated the Burmese refugees wonderfully. They were given money and accommodation. She went to the Calcutta office of Steel Brothers, told them who she was and where her husband worked and was immediately given financial assistance. Do not imagine that my mother had a change of heart about the dog-Indians as she says all this. When she talks about how kind the Indians were, she means the British Indians, like the tea planters in Assam and the civil servants in charge of refugees in Calcutta. 'They were extraordinarily good to us in India.

We refugees got first refusal for jobs. Someone arriving from Burma could find work if they wanted it, secretaries, nurses, clerks, anything, but then they were dealing with an educated class of people. The Anglo-Burmese had all had a proper education. They had skills,' said my mother.

Chico – the maligned Chico who had married her brother-in-law Peter – was also in Calcutta at the time and offered my mother and sister help, but she was a Seventh Day Adventist and my mother was a little wary of being converted. She wanted to go to a hill station, somewhere like Dehra Dun which turned out to be my birth place, but there was a problem. Where would she and the baby stay? 'In a boarding-house,' replied stage manager O'Leary. My mother was mystified. She had never heard of a boarding-house. They didn't exist in Burma. Apart from the Strand Hotel and the Pegu Club in Rangoon, there were no hotels anywhere else.

'But suppose you didn't have relatives or friends in the town you were visiting, what did you do then?' I asked. I should have known better. My mother can make friends with anyone. She cannot sit down in a bus or train or stand in a supermarket without talking to the person next to her. It's a compulsion. Within seconds she will have told her companion where she is going and why and by the end of the ride or the queue which may well have only lasted five minutes the stranger will be familiar with all the relevant details of our family history.

There was the famous occasion in 1951 when my mother was travelling by train from Hertfordshire to London. She mentioned to the woman sitting opposite her in the carriage that she had just left her children in boarding-school and she herself would be living abroad in Borneo for two years. And why was that, asked the woman on the train. 'Well,' said my mother, 'it's a long story.' Mind you, that had never stopped her before. She was joining her husband in Borneo for a two-year stint and had left her two small children in boarding-schools where they were perfectly entitled to stay for the holidays, too, but it would be so much nicer for them if they could stay with a friendly English family. Unfortunately, having recently arrived in England, she didn't know many people so the poor children would just have to get on as best they could.

I have only a dim memory of Mrs Fletcher, as the woman on the train turned out to be. She was a thin, hard-faced harridan. She was also a smooth operator. Within half an hour of telling my mother she lived in Margate and had a daughter of twelve called Angela, and would be delighted to act as guardian to the two temporary orphans, my mother had handed over her cheque-book and given Mrs Fletcher *carte blanche* with her bank account. It was a short-lived arrangement. Jenny and I spent the first Christmas holiday that my mother was away in Margate. Angela was a bully, Mrs Fletcher a shrew, they were both shopaholics and by the end of three weeks my mother's account had been drained. At the beginning of the Easter term Reverend Mother wrote to my mother in Borneo. In her opinion Susan and Jennifer should stay in Tring until she returned and that was the end of our Margate excursion. My mother didn't learn from this salutary experience: she continued to make instant friends, some admittedly turned out to be diamonds, the rest only wanted to take her for a ride. But you can see why she never needed a boarding-house, she would always make friends with someone.

So she went to Dehra Dun, stayed in a boarding-house with the baby, and at some point joined the Women's Army Corps India where she had a jolly war walking out with British officers. My father had the occasional leave with her and, despite what she says about being fed up with his uncouth Burmese ways, they must have had a few good times, because I was born in the army hospital in Mhow, shortly before my mother left the army and went back to Burma.

The war was over. My father returned to Steel Brothers and on the face of it they were a typical Anglo-Burmese couple, with two children, living the marooned life of all colonial Anglos. My mother's reason for leaving Burma in 1947 was to get medical treatment for my sister, but even if Jenny hadn't been going blind she would have found some excuse to leave. 'I was never one of them,' she maintains. 'My mother always said I would leave Burma and live in England.'

5

Under an English Heaven

Everything I have written up to now is hearsay. We are now entering the realms of personal recollection. I have always had a brilliant memory. I passed exams not because I was naturally intelligent but because I could remember everything, facts, figures, dates, great chunks of poetry, which always impressed the examiners. My first memories of England are not of home but of school. I went to boarding-school when I was three. It hadn't been planned that way. My mother had booked a place for my sister at Bradwin Girls' College in Sevenoaks and had duly paid a term's fees in advance. She had even bought the uniform. But once in London, the consultant at Moorfields Eye Hospital made it clear my sister's sight was too poor for her to attend a normal school. Instead she was sent off to a school for the partially sighted in Exeter. So it was up to me to fill the unrefundable fees-paid-in-advance place, and the uniform which was five sizes too big. My mother has always been thrifty by nature. She put six-inch hems on my gym-slips and took me down to Kent on the train.

There were two headmistresses at Bradwin College, spinster sisters whom we called Big Miss Tocker and Little Miss Tocker. Big Miss Tocker wore black, Little Miss Tocker wore brown, they both wore sensible shoes and hair nets and smelled of mothballs. Being the youngest in the school by a good three years, I enjoyed roughly the same status as a regimental goat. I was the Bradwin College Mascot. As the smallest as well as the youngest pupil in this, and probably any other, school in history, I was petted and pampered outrageously. I spent most of my school life sitting on either one of the Miss Tockers' ample laps eating chocolates. I didn't go to formal lessons. I was personally tutored like a Victorian child with her governess – better still, two governesses – and, not surprisingly under this hothouse care, I thrived. It was this grounding I believe that made me such a smartass in my later school life.

I stayed at Sevenoaks for two years not so much because my mother didn't want me at home, but because she was busy trying to make a life for herself in England, as I shall come to later. But let me finish with my early schooling. Having abandoned the comfortable laps of Big Miss Tocker and Little Miss Tocker, I went to a private primary school in Harrow called Whitegates.

The one indelible memory I have of Whitegates was the morning I was sent home from assembly. Nothing to do with bad conduct – I was much too nervous to behave badly and only wanted to ingratiate myself with the others. It was my uniform. In summer Whitegates girls wore bottle-green and white striped dresses, the usual skimpy things offered by school outfitters. My mother went there to buy me a dress, was horrified at the cost and said she could run up one exactly like it for quarter of the price.

I've said she was always a brilliant dressmaker. So we marched out of the Whitegates outfitters and instead went to a shop that sold material. We bought a length of green and white striped cotton, it wasn't quite bottle-green, my mother said bottle-green was very unflattering for small girls. It was more of an emerald green and the stripes were marginally wider than regulation but never mind, my mother insisted it was far more becoming. I should explain that as a family we didn't have many ordinary books on the bookshelves. My sister had her huge braille volumes and the rest of the space was taken up with Butterick and Simplicity paper patterns from which she made all our clothes. Post-war rationing still prevailed but she never let a minor irritation like clothing coupons stand in the way of her self-expression. We spent most Saturday mornings at Sopers in Harrow looking through the pattern books and if my mother was feeling extravagant she would spend an extra sixpence and buy a Vogue designer pattern. The pattern she bought for my school uniform was approximately the same as the school but approximations are no good for school. The collar was deeper, the skirt fuller, the sleeves puffier, the sash wider and so generous in its length that you could tie it in a big double bow at the back like a Victorian bustle. My mother was delighted with the result and asked friends to confirm her opinion that it was far prettier than the usual school uniform. I was doubtful. I looked at myself in the glass and saw not a simple schoolgirl but a strange, foreign-looking child in a party dress.

'Isn't it a bit too good for school,' I ventured.

'Nonsense,' said my mother and packed me off. Of course it was a disaster. Amongst the long lines of pupils at morning assembly I stood out like a sore thumb. I was sent home to change. I wept, my mother fumed, but school rules were school rules.

She unleashed her creative skills on me out of school instead. She bought the sort of patterns only girls built like scaffolding would have looked good in. I was now well into my puppy-fat stage but my mother, blind to my defects, stitched lime-green satin Bermuda shorts (before they became fashionable) and matching skinny tops for me to wear to the shops. I sometimes sat in my room feigning illness rather than be seen in these home-made extravagances.

While I settled in my various schools my mother was having to survive in a new country and a new life. She arrived in the worst winter England had suffered since records began, with two small children, nowhere to live and no job. She was not at all fazed. She had always been resourceful and energetic, not characteristics normally associated with Burmese women, at least not the ones we met in London through contacts she had been given in Burma. They were timid and retiring and let their husbands do the talking and decision-making. In England my mother had no husband so she made all the decisions herself. She managed to jump every queue at Moorfields Eye Hospital, and Mr Cross, the consultant who saw my sister, waived his fees. My mother wasn't on the scrounge, she was loaded, thanks to the generosity of my father who gave her twenty pounds a week. No, she got her way because she was naturally charming. She didn't put it on to impress. This charm coupled with her stunning looks opened most doors and clearly seduced the man who interviewed her for her first job as a secretary in a leather wholesalers. She couldn't type, she couldn't do shorthand, but I can imagine exactly how she got the job: a room full of applicants, pasty-faced women from Harrow in drab clothes bought with ration coupons, and there in the middle of them the exotic little figure of Marjorie McHarg in her brilliant feathers made by the verandah *derzi* in Burma and quite unsuitable for the bitter English winter. She must have looked like a jay among sparrows. She never wore what the English call classic clothes. She liked bright colours, spots and stripes and buttons and bows and frills and bits, all worn together.

She was someone who could never pass unnoticed in a crowd.

So she took a secretarial crash course at night school and kept the job for four years. She once showed me the leather wholesalers. It was grim, near Wembley, in what we would now call a light industrial estate. I like to visualise her going to work in Perivale every morning click-clacking off for the bus in her high heels. She wore a lot of make-up in those days, she says, and it seemed to do the trick, for she had a stream of male admirers whom my sister and I called Uncle this and that. I don't remember the make-up, except for the lipstick which she put on in front of her dressing-table mirror, one of those elaborate affairs with three hinging mirrors and lots of pink and blue roses round the frames. She wore a lot of rouge, too, patting it into place on her high cheek-bones with a small tortoiseshell brush which had been my sister's first baby hairbrush. When she brushed her thick, glossy hair with her ivory-backed brushes she did it the opposite way to English people then, putting the brush under her hair behind her neck and brushing it upwards to make it stick out like a halo.

We were in our first proper house in England, 34 Christchurch Avenue, and my mother was still feeling her way. Most of our friends were Burma contacts. If by some chance my mother met an English person and invited them home we made a special effort. And if anyone was kind to us, even to the extent of telling us where the nearest post office was, my mother would repay them handsomely, maybe with a gold sovereign (part of Charlie Lloyd's hoard), or some of her silver apostle spoons. She was touchingly generous to visitors. She said she got it from her mother who economised with her family but pushed the boat out for guests. If Grannie had a wonderful piece of fish she would always say, 'Who can we invite round to share it, it's too good just for the family.' My mother is the same.

Our next house on Woodcock Hill was definitely a step up the social ladder. There were hardly any immigrants like us which made my mother something of a talking point in the neighbourhood. We were invited to tea by the Clarks across the road and even though someone later told us Ron Clark had made all his money from scrap iron it didn't matter. He was English, his wife was English, his children were fat and spotty and irredeemably plain but they were English and we respected them for it.

Our closest friends lived in the road that ran at right-angles to Woodcock Hill and we knew them because their back garden abutted ours and I and their only daughter Janet had become best friends over the garden fence. Uncle Joe, Janet's father, worked for the gas board and Auntie Vera, his wife, had a passion for ballroom dancing. Her favourite word was 'adjudicator', she went in for foxtrot and *paso doble* competitions and made flamboyant besequinned ball dresses in which to take part. She and my mother had an instant rapport because Auntie Vera was as fanatical a dressmaker as she. Everything in Auntie Vera's house was home-made, from the oven gloves to the matching tea cosy and kitchen curtains. She and my mother would vie to make things out of left overs; sometimes my mother went way over the top.

On the occasion I remember most vividly she used every remnant from her glory hole to make a party dress for herself. It was for some smart do we had been asked to and for weeks before, you could hear her whirring away in the bedroom. Emerging at last from upstairs she announced happily to us all, 'I've used everything, the frill round that old dressing-table we had at 34 Christchurch, the bathroom curtains Auntie Winnie gave us and the rest of the purple net from Jenny's party dress.'

Being a child used to dressing-up boxes I thought she looked magnificent. When we arrived at the party everyone stopped talking and just stared. You couldn't blame them. My mother's dress was a dog's dinner, combining every style, colour and texture. The top had milkmaid overtones *à la* Marie Antoinette, there was a layer of white lace around the knee (those were the bathroom curtains), followed by two flounces of purple net, some sprigged muslin from the dressing-table frill and finally a border of chintz, originally bought to cover an armchair in the sitting-room. It was my favourite Burmese aunt, Auntie Patsy, who played the small boy to Hans Andersen's naked emperor. 'Marjorie, what on earth do you think you look like?' she said pointing a long cigarette holder disdainfully at the layers of lace and chintz and purple net. 'Talk about mutton dressed as lamb.'

Auntie Patsy was an old friend of my mother's from teachers' training college in Rangoon. She had married an Englishman called Clifford Bailey, a stores manager for Steel Brothers. When I was small I thought Patsy and Cliff were the most glamorous couple I'd ever seen. Patsy was duskily beautiful and talked with a film-star drawl. She wore dark glasses all the time and always had a cigarette smouldering at the end of a cigarette holder. She smoked eighty a day, still does. They had a cottage in Shoreham-by-Sea, when Shoreham was still a seaside village.

They threw what I imagined were the sort of parties Scott and Zelda Fitzgerald went to in the South of France. Lots of people, lots of drink, and lots and lots of loud calypso music with Patsy and Cliff swaying lazily to the beat, glass in one hand, cigarette holder in the other. It was Auntie Patsy who gave me my first culinary advice. Bake in brandy, boil in gin. She used to drink gin from a teacup and saucer while the rest of us were drinking PG Tips. They had no children. My mother told me that Patsy too had trekked out of Burma after Pearl Harbor. She was pregnant at the time and had lost the baby on the way and had never been able to have another. That may have accounted for the permanently sad expression in Auntie's eyes and why she wore dark glasses.

We were always very friendly with Patsy and Cliff, I had a crush on one of Uncle Cliff's nephews, and it came as a bit of a shock one day to hear my mother say that Uncle Cliff was a bit common. Socially speaking, she said, a stores manager was a pretty lowly job. It was puzzling because when we lived in Kenton we were quite happy to socialise with Uncle Joe who read meters for the Gas Board and when he ate stew would mop up the gravy dribbles from his face with a piece of bread and then eat the bread.

My mother's pronouncement upon Cliff's social standing came after she had left my father and married David, whom she considered to be a cut above every other white man. Not that Auntie Patsy herself was spared the lash of her tongue. When my stepfather lost all his money in the Hampshire farming venture my mother got a teaching job to boost the family finances. Her Rangoon diploma was recognised in England. She always hated teaching although she was very good at it. She would get impatient with the ones who only wanted to disrupt the lesson and knew cunning ways of pinching them where it didn't show. Behind their ears was one. But, she said, at least she was able to get the job, whereas poor Patsy, also a trained teacher, never even got past the first interview because she was so dark.

'I think she must have a bit of Indian blood in her somewhere,' said my mother, the colourways expert. 'Her name before she married Cliff was Gonzales. She claims to be Portuguese but anyone can see she is Indian.'

Until she met my stepfather and learned differently, my mother considered our house at 126 Woodcock Hill the apotheosis of all that was perfect. It had a garden front and back and an oak tree of its own on the pavement outside the front gate. It was superior to other houses, not just for its bay windows upstairs and down, but because the hall was

L-shaped so that you did not see the staircase immediately but came upon it only after turning the corner. This was considered very gracious indeed. The house was full of Burmese bric-à-brac which excited the neighbours no end. We had a fire screen made of teak with two curved ivory tusks on either side and a set of six carved dancing girls, also made of ivory, on glass shelves either side of the fire. We had ornaments shaped like apples made of silver so thin and delicate that if you squeezed them gently in your hand they would crush. We had a big, square, green-and-gold velvet three-piece suite with ornate fringing, and Persian rugs, and felt every bit as good as the scrap dealer across the road. My mother was still working in Perivale, click-clacking off to work every morning in her high heels and make-up, but in the evenings old friends from Christchurch Avenue would come round to admire our superior residence. 'It's the only house with the oak tree outside,' my mother would say proudly.

And then everything changed. My mother told my sister and me that she would have to go away for two years to be with Daddy. He had been transferred to a forestry operation in Borneo. I don't know why she went. Maybe she just wanted a change from the cold weather. Surely she couldn't have thought she would find her pale-skinned prince in the jungle of Borneo? My sister was sent to board at a school for the blind in Tring, I was enrolled in the convent down the road. The plans for our holidays were fluid until that encounter with Mrs Fletcher on the train. After the Margate débâcle my sister and I spent holidays in the convent, along with a small band of foreign refugee orphans.

But we weren't orphans. Once a month my mother sent a parcel of goodies from Sarawak containing the most wonderful items. Huge tins of Quality Street chocolates, sometimes slightly mouldy, and others containing strange foreign sweets with delicate foreign flavours. Every month when my parcel arrived I'd be surrounded by 'friends' asking me to share boxes. As well as sweets there were ornaments, funny little glass chickens and porcupines which became vital to my personal happiness as a child, estranged as I was from my mother. But best of all in those monthly parcels were the dolls' clothes my mother had made for my collection. Whatever the tailor in Borneo made for her, she would make an exact replica in miniature for one of my dollies, perfect to the last frill and tuck. I would sometimes come across a pin in the hem of a tiny dress which my mother had forgotten to take out in her hurry to get the things finished and despatched.

When she returned to England with my stepfather in tow, she told me that it was actually David who had sent the parcels to us, not her. I don't believe it. I think it was just an attempt on her part to make us love our new stepfather more. The exact circumstances under which they met are clothed in mystery. David Thomas James was a bachelor of forty-four when the exotic Mrs Marjorie McHarg arrived at the logging camp in Borneo to join her husband, one of his employees. It must have been a cloak-and-dagger affair for, just as thirty years earlier my grandfather, William Thomas Townley, had failed to get promotion because of his native attachment, the big noises in the Bombay Burmah Trading Company did not encourage their directors to go native. My mother reminisces about romantic walks in the jungle under the flame trees with David carrying her over puddles, straight out of a Mills and Boon blockbuster. But where on earth was my father when all this romance was going on? All I know is that my mother came home the colour of delta mud, swept me from the familiar and loving arms of the Sisters of St Francis de Sales who had been my surrogate parents for two years, and took me home to Woodcock Hill which had been rented to a diplomatic family while we were away. That was the first time I met my future stepfather.

He was what she had been waiting for, hoping for, ever since she and Dolly Corrie, in the care of Mummy Fairclough at St Matthew's, had vowed only to be friends with pretty girls, marry Englishmen and live happily ever after. I was too small to notice how substantially my life changed when we left Kenton for Hampshire. I don't remember being with my father but then she was never really with him. He worked in Burma, she lived in London. When he came on leave they went on holiday, once to Nice from where they brought back tiny straw baskets with Nice embroidered on the side, and once to Scotland. And now instead of my well-built, good-looking father, here was a new Uncle, smaller, slighter, fine-looking in a quiet way, in fact not like anyone I'd ever met before. Well he was white, all white, for a start, not like the usual Anglo-Burmese brand of uncles that came round to visit. He wasn't smooth like Uncle Neal the salesman or gregarious and chatty like Uncle Cliff, and even to my seven-year-old eyes I could see that he was from a different planet to Uncle Joe from the Gas Board.

The one thing everyone said about David James was that he was a gentleman. Funny that, because he certainly wasn't born one. His father was a Welsh Methodist missionary and, by all accounts, almost sadistically strict with his five children. David, the eldest of four sons, was born in the Cook Islands where James senior had started a mission school. David, like his brothers John and Bill, was educated at Eltham College near Blackheath where most of the pupils were the children of missionaries. One of my stepfather's closest friends at school was Eric Liddle, later to become an olympic runner. We never knew this until the film *Chariots of Fire* was such a success. David, a mild man not much given to chat or self-promotion, said to no one in particular that he knew Eric Liddle was a good runner because they'd sneak out to Lewisham to see a film after prep and Liddle would say, 'Come on, run faster or we'll miss the start,' and my stepfather who was much smaller would pant and say, 'It's no good I can't,' and Liddle would seize his hand and drag him after him. They never missed the start of a film.

There was a sticky moment the first week that my mother and her new love arrived home. My father turned up. Unexpectedly. David James had to scarper and the acrimony began – who was to blame? My mother of course, it was all her fault. I love her more than life but I have every sympathy for my father who was blameless and whose only fault was that he couldn't say 'froth' properly. It was public knowledge in the Bombay Burmah that David James, Jamie, had gone off with an Anglo-Burmese and if he had not opted to take early retirement he would probably have been asked to resign. The idea was to sink all his pension in a smallholding and become a gentleman farmer, and to this end he and my mother started looking at farmhouses.

I was still in Kenton, living with my father and going to the school where those older boys stung my knees with nettles. Having survived that ordeal I then came home and spent the rest of the evening listening to my father ranting against my evil mother. I think he must have gone slightly off his head, he kept calling David a murderer. If he saw me writing letters to my mother he would snatch them up and tear them to pieces. I was not to utter her name or write it in his house. I have this peculiar memory of coming home from school and going straight over to one of the big green-and-gold velvet armchairs, where I put my satchel on the floor and laid my head on the seat, swung my legs up and stood on my head for half an hour while my father sat on the sofa ranting.

The objects of this vitriol had by now bought and moved into their new home. It was my mother's choice and had my stepfather been a more decisive and forceful man he would have told her it was a totally unsuitable house to farm from, but he was not and my mother had made up her mind in any case. It was a stone hunting lodge originally built for the Earl of Warwick. I can almost hear my mother reading this out from the estate agent's prospectus, and savouring those glorious words. If it had gone on to say it was made of mud with a thatched roof and no water my mother would probably have had it just the same. It was certainly a pretty little house, set in a Hampshire wood with a hundred acres of surrounding woodlands, but for someone trying to start a small pig farm it wasn't really suitable. No matter. My mother wanted it so she got it. Besides, having been shown round the two reception rooms both featuring the same velvet wallpaper as used in Warwick Castle, the original Adam fireplaces etc., it did not matter a whit that there were only two bedrooms upstairs and not a single outbuilding, not even a garage. Dwe would clear the land and build pig houses and tractor sheds and a road to reach them.

He had lots of pension money from the Bombay Burmah and, accordingly, my mother opened an account at Peter Jones and set to work furnishing North Lodge. To this day, thirty years after we left North Lodge, she will still clasp her hands together and say that the colour scheme for the drawing-room in that first Hampshire house was the most wonderful thing ever devised. She said she remembers people coming into it and blinking they were so amazed. They would have been. The Earl of Warwick's wallpaper was a pale peach which toned pleasingly with the grey marble of the Adam fireplace. These in turn, my mother opined, would go beautifully with a fitted cherry-red carpet, lime-green velvet curtains, a pair of acid-yellow armchairs and a scarlet sofa that turned into a bed. We had some interesting pictures, an oil painting of a cancan dancer, one leg raised while the flounced skirt fell round her garters and frilly pants, and of course the picture of the Shan princess whose father, the Saw Bwa, helped my grandmother when the Japanese arrested her. There was a piano and a writing desk and later my mother added her own *pièce de résistance*.

She had come across a single carved mahogany bedpost about four foot high, the sort of thing people have propped in a corner of their garden shed, too precious to chuck out, too useless to do anything with. But my mother had a plan. She went to a garden shop and bought a huge terracotta flowerpot. She found a circular piece of wood, cut a hole in the middle, stuck the bedpost into the pot through this and topped it off with a huge flock-velvet lampshade. The work was not yet finished. She painted glue all over the surface of the pot and threw handfuls of rice at it as if she were making a pebble-dash wall. She then painted the whole thing gold. It stood tall, burnished and oddly menacing, next to the writing desk and was just something else for the visitors to gasp over.

It was not only bedposts she couldn't bring herself to throw away. She could find a use for just about anything. Play-school teachers creating dolls' houses out of yoghurt cartons and space shuttles from empty loo rolls had nothing on my mother for ingenuity. Take another unusual decorative feature of our North Lodge drawing-room. It was a leather cannon case filled with corn on the cob. We had them for supper, biting the corn off the cob in circles. Why throw the cob away, reasoned my thrifty mother? She washed and dried them, they looked like small loofas, painted them in brilliant primary colours with children's poster paint, stuck them on the ends of long canes, twined green paper round the stems to resemble leaves and arranged them gracefully in the cannon case.

'Goodness, how ingenious you are Marjorie,' visitors would gasp admiringly if they were Burmese, horrified, if they were the local nobs.

That was what my mother liked best. Entertaining the local gentry on their terms and on her newly acquired terms, in the dining-room of her tiny stone hunting lodge built originally for the Earl of Warwick etc., etc. We had caterers because my mother wasn't confident about her cooking. She was good at stew and curries but Hampshire gentry couldn't be expected to eat stew and wouldn't understand curry. So the caterers made cooked chicken in cream sauce and trifle with sherry and my mother polished the Mappin and Webb salt cellars till you could see your face in them. Sometimes I would be asked to put salt in the small dark-blue glass containers that sat inside the silver cases. My stepfather would take it all in his stride but my mother worked feverishly to get everything as pukka as it had been 'out East', as everyone in the area referred to anywhere east of Brindisi.

Getting things right meant calling drinks by their proper club names, a Stinger not whisky and soda, a gimlet not gin and lime – and it had to be Rose's Lime Juice for a real gimlet. I would be in bed when the guests arrived but I could hear the odd snatch of conversation. My mother often opened with 'Well of course when you've been used to being out East . . .' and to those big clumsy horsy Hampshire people it must have conjured up pictures of white dinner-jackets and polo and delicate oriental dancing girls. If she had told them about Ko Ko and his *stik lak* turning to dust in his bankrupt go-downs or crow duty, they would have looked bewildered but, of course, she never did. They understood Jamie perfectly well. He was a gent and they admired him for bagging this wonderfully exotic little wife but they didn't want to pry too much into her background. They couldn't have, even if they wanted. My mother only let out edited snippets.

To start with she wore perfectly normal clothes, if a little theatrical, but as she became more sure of herself she took to wearing Burmese costume to her dinner parties. Upstairs in my bedroom I could hear Pauline Baldock's squeal, 'Oh Marjorie how absolutely delightful, but can you really walk in that without it all coming unwrapped?' Then my mother might show them her party trick, the one she demonstrated at Women's Institutes, where she would unwrap her *longyi* at the waist and hoik it up over her blouse and under her armpits the same modest way Burmese village maidens did when they washed in the river.

North Lodge was an appendage of what everyone called the Big House, a Victorian monstrosity complete with towers and peacocks, called Hollycombe House. When we moved in to our lodge we were informed that Mrs Boycott, who had worked for the previous owners of Hollycombe, was prepared to help us out twice a week. Mrs Boycott duly arrived to size us up. She was small, fierce and sixty. One glance at the golden rice-bowl lamp and the corn cobs in the cannon case was enough. She summed up the situation, knew that she would have sole authority in our household, and she did. We used to clean the house the day before Mrs Boycott arrived. As she worked her way round polishing and dusting, Mrs Boycott would talk about Her Ladyship. We soon knew about Her Ladyship's preferences regarding the upkeep of silver, china, linen and glass. Her Ladyship never used anything on the beds but pure Irish linen, monogrammed of course. Mrs Boycott had supervised the application of the monograms. Her Ladyship had had only Waterford Crystal in her drinks cabinet, Her Ladyship only used beeswax on her antique furniture.

Mrs Boycott lived in a converted outhouse nearer to the Big House than ours, only half a mile from us but she was collected and delivered to do her dusting twice a week. Next to her lived a man who worked for the Hollycombe estate referred to by Mrs Boycott as Mr L'Emont. She pronounced it with an exaggerated French accent to rhyme with Mont Blanc. We followed suit calling, 'Good morning Mr L'Emont' as we passed him on the road. It was only by chance that someone later told us his name was Lemon. Mrs Boycott was with us for five years and fortunately retired before we had to sack her because the farm was going steadily broke.

It had a brief golden age when porkers and baconers were sent squealing off to market every Friday and every Monday a letter like a school report arrived to say that they were all straight As in terms of optimum weight, leanness and condition. That was the time when we knew every pig by sight and all the sows. In the end we had twenty sows to whom my mother had given Burmese names, all except Lady Luck, the first to step on to our land. The rest were called things like Ma Chi (Miss Love), Ma Nya (Miss Black) and Ma Nu (Miss Tender), after my paternal grandmother, a small revenge by her daughter-in-law.

We had head-hunted the local taxi driver from Liphook station to be our pigman and Joe renamed all the sows after his sisters, Peggy, Doris, Gladys, Lilly and so on. It took a year to build the farm, including its steep access road. In retrospect, that is why it went under so quickly. They spent far too much of David's capital setting the thing up. It would have been much better to buy a ready-made farm and if the Earl of Warwick, or any other convenient aristocrat, had had one for sale we probably would have done so. But my mother had fallen in love with North Lodge and the die was cast. To give her her due she worked as much for the farm as the two men.

After the first three sows had arrived and been installed in their pens, my parents went to Denmark at the invitation of a pig breeder, to try and learn the nuts and bolts of the business. I call them my parents, much to my real father's fury, but it is a mouthful to keep on saying stepfather. David had no farming education at all, he had joined the Bombay Burmah shortly after leaving school and elephants were his only acquaintance with livestock. They spent two days in an enormous industrial complex watching lively porkers and baconers being led into a huge unit at one end and packs of streaky bacon and sausages emerging at the other. My parents watched fascinated, asked questions, made notes and at last their Danish hosts asked how many pigs they had. Three said my mother. Three hundred, three thousand, asked the Dane. No, just three said my mother, Lady Luck, Ma Chi and Ma Nya.

If a traditional pig farmer had come to look at us, I don't think he would have recognised much of what he saw. We had the right equipment, a tractor which I could drive at twelve, farrowing huts, fattening pens. It was more my parents' style of farming that would have flummoxed him. My mother was the driving force behind all the decisions. If she read somewhere that pigs thrived better on skimmed milk than conventional pig nuts she would go ahead and order a tank and a weekly delivery of stinking stuff would arrive. Skimmed milk sitting in a tank the size of a swimming pool goes off quickly and the smell is something else. We would ladle it out to the pigs in buckets and when the level dropped it was quite a tricky operation getting it out. One day my mother, leaning over the side with her bucket, lost her balance and fell in. She said afterwards that it may not have smelled great but it did wonders for dry skin.

Turning her back on my father, Woodcock Hill and the rest of her early life also meant losing touch with all our North London friends. It was one thing to have tea with the rich scrap dealer in his large house while we were in Kenton, but he would definitely not pass muster in Hampshire. If Mrs Boycott ever got wind of it we would have been sunk. The only people we kept in touch with from Kenton were Auntie Vera, Uncle Joe and my best friend Janet. They were always welcome, provided they gave enough advance notice, so that my mother could organise a sort of social quarantine arrangement in the house while they were incumbent. Mrs Boycott was given time off.

So why did my mother invite them? To be fair to her she did get on well with Auntie Vera, a woman with whom you could commiserate for hours about anything from an earthquake in Tehran to the price of pot noodles. There was nothing Auntie Vera liked more than a good moan and my mother too is partial to a bit of healthy complaint. She would far rather discuss someone's bad points than their assets, unless of course they're family when they can do no wrong. But the main reason we asked them was that they were useful. The farm needed fencing, Uncle Joe was built like an ox and would work until dark hammering in fence posts. And while he was doing that, Auntie Vera would take over in the kitchen, allowing my mother time to get on with her dressmaking or her craft work. The latest preoccupation was patchwork. Someone had given her a bag of mixed silk remnants from a tailor who made up jockeys' colours. My mother was now making jockey silk patchwork quilts for her children, and anyone else who wanted one. There was an awful lot of silk in the bag. We could only feel a bit grateful to Auntie Vera for her cooking because she was what people call a plain cook. I once asked her how to cook a lamb chop. 'You put it in the oven for two hours with a bit of fat and water,' she replied.

We lived in Hampshire for nine happy years as far as I was concerned. I had no idea about finance. I had left a small private school to go to ballet school, having been told by the local dance teacher that I had a career on the stage. Suddenly looking different paid dividends. If they needed a leprechaun or a leopard or any other character that didn't fit the peaches-and-cream mould, I was the obvious choice. I got used to wearing false whiskers and different sorts of tails but I was dispirited because all I wanted was to be a classical prima ballerina. In the holidays my parents' dinner-party friends, hearing about my theatrical ambitions, would look knowingly at each other and smile understandingly. There were always parts for exotics and weirdos. But at sixteen I was bulky and bolshi and as my hopes of becoming a cygnet in the nearest *corps de ballet* faded, so did my acceptance of being cast as yet another goblin in the end-of-term production. The dilemma was neatly solved by my being expelled for smoking, nothing more terrible than Woodbines but the free-booting, swinging 'sixties had only just begun and I was despatched to Guildford poly to get my A levels. Apart from playing one of the Chinese laundrymen in *Aladdin*, I don't remember feeling self-conscious about my appearance then or at any time throughout my university life.

Trinity College Dublin had a reputation for hearties – ex-public-school chaps who played rugger and wore tweeds. There was one on my course called Clifford something, Tiffy to closer friends, who was TCD's equivalent to 'Jennifer's Diary'. What Tiffy didn't know about pedigree wasn't worth knowing. He went to bed with *Burke's Peerage*. He could determine a person's class on sight. He said it had much to do with their shoes. The way they spoke merely confirmed his spontaneous evaluation. I wondered why he needed to do all this. 'Because it influences the way I treat them,' said Tiffy. And how did he evaluate me? 'Oh, you're different. You don't count because you're foreign,' he said.

It counted when I spent a sabbatical in the States at the University of Colorado. I'd managed to swing an assistantship to the English professor there, even though I was still an undergraduate, and charming as he was, I know I was a disappointment to him because I didn't look the pukka English part. Same with my room-mate Charlene from Chicago. When she got to know me better she told me she was shocked when she first saw me. 'I'd heard I was rooming with someone from London. I was expecting a typical English Rose and got you,' she said. Invariably, I was introduced thus: 'This is Susan. She's from England. She doesn't look it but wait till she opens her mouth.'

Every foreign student at the University of Colorado was allotted a campus friend, a senior who would show them the ropes. Mine was an East Coast WASP called Roger who reacted in the same way as Charlene, except he said patronisingly he had always fancied dark-skinned girls. When men make that sort of remark you're supposed to feel grateful that you make up in novelty value for not holding your fork properly or being able to talk about Henley. Roger wasn't so excited about my colour after a few of us spent the week of the spring semester break in Acapulco. I tan alarmingly quickly. After seven days under the grilling Mexican sun I was the colour of antique mahogany and had trouble convincing immigration at San Antonio that I was truly the owner of a British passport and not just another wetback trying to cross illegally.

It wasn't much better back home in my first job. In Blackburn on my first newspaper, I was treated with ubiquitous suspicion, as much for my social standing as for my appearance. Women graduates pursuing a career weren't exactly thick on the ground in this run-down Lancashire mill town, and there weren't many girls over twenty-one like me not married. At lunch-times I went dancing at the Mecca with sixteen-year-old Marilyn who worked as a Telesales operator on the *Evening Telegraph*. At night I sat by myself in my bed-sitter and planned how I could get out of signing my indentures contracting me to the newspaper for two years.

After a couple of months I got a break. The editor devised a column for me under the banner 'Sue's Scene – Sue from the South takes a fresh look at us northerners'. I was despatched to write purple prose about bingo parlours and the fruit-and-veg market. I had a by-line photograph which contrived to make me look as if 'from the South' meant somewhere south of the Sahara. I did look very foreign. The fashion in those days was back-combed hair, the higher the better. I looked like Susie Wong in a busby. When I telephoned to say I was coming to write about so and so for my 'fresh look' purposes, I'd hear people put their hands over the mouthpiece and whisper, 'It's that toffee-nosed chink from t'*Telegraph*.'

Some took it harder than others. It was the *Telegraph*'s long-standing practice at Christmas to have a raffle every Saturday with £100 worth of festive goodies for the winner and someone representing the paper's Christmas fairy to deliver it. That year I was the Christmas fairy and pretty strange I looked too with my hottentot hairdo under a tinsel crown. I knocked on the front door of the winner's two-up, two-down terraced house in the Whalley Road, wand in one hand, hamper of good things in the other.

'Congratulations, Mr Johnson,' I cried. 'I've come to tell you that . . .'

'We'll 'ave none of your mumbo jumbo in this house,' replied the householder sharply. 'Bugger off' and slammed the door.

And then at last I gravitated to Fleet Street and a job on the Diary of the *Evening Standard* where I got used to being called Kowloon Lucy and even got a small scoop by becoming the first and only reporter to penetrate the Chinese legation which had briefly run amok. Pickaxe-wielding diplomats had been seen in Portland Place protesting about some capitalist infringement of their liberties, after which they had barred the doors, refusing access to all comers. For a couple of days the trench-coated hacks from all the national papers had laid siege to the legation in Portland Place but no one had managed to get in and seek an audience. 'Why not send Kowloon Lucy to try her luck? She is one of them after all,' suggested someone in the *Standard* office. The rest, as they say, is history. I knocked on the door of the legation watched by the mocking eyes of my colleagues, I was admitted, handed a copy of Chairman Mao's *Little Red Book* and treated to a fifteen-minute lecture on the evils of imperialism by a Mao-suited official. Given the choice, I'd have stayed on the *Standard* Diary for ever, I felt I had reached the pinnacle of my journalistic career, I thought I had died and gone to heaven. I loved the job, racing round London interviewing celebrities, writing off-the-cuff paragraphs about new exhibitions, champagne receptions for visiting Hollywood stars, first nights. Alas it was short-lived. Three months into the job my old Blackburn editor lodged a formal complaint to the *Standard* editor that I had not completed my two years' indentures in the provinces and was therefore not entitled under the NUJ guidelines to work for a National newspaper. I went before a disciplinary tribunal consisting of the London correspondent of TASS (the Soviet News Agency), a motherly soul from *Woman's Own* and somebody else – I forget who – and was cautioned against showing my face in the capital until I'd got my two provincial years' apprenticeship under my belt.

The penalty was harsh. I was fined fifty pounds, booted off the *Standard* and ordered back to the provinces to complete my indentures. None of the other Diary reporters had even heard of the provinces, let alone set foot in them. They were old Etonians to a man. I at least had six months in Blackburn notched up. To this day, I have a nagging suspicion that had I been called Emily Ponsonby Giles and looked the English Rose, the editor would have fought to keep me on the staff. But he didn't and I left, feeling short-changed and embittered. This is not supposed to be a blow-by-blow account of my career – suffice to say I got myself a job on the *Manchester Evening News*, then sneaked back into Fleet Street on the *Daily Sketch*, went to Tehran and worked on an English-language paper, nearly married a diplomat out there and finally came to marry my first husband, Hugh. I wanted, like my mother, to marry the perfect Englishman and in Hugh I though I'd found the answer. Public-school educated, tall, good-looking, arrogant and something in the City. What neither I nor my mother, who naturally relished the prospect of such a thoroughbred son-in-law, had bargained for was that other English characteristic, eccentricity. How could any of us foresee that a decade on, Hugh would throw in his job, abandon four children under seven and devote the rest of his life to running marathons. But that's another story.

6

Rangoon Relatives

It is now 1985 and I have decided to drop in on my Burmese relatives on my way back from covering the Royal Tour of China. It will be nothing short of a diplomatic mission for I have two distinct sets of relatives to visit.

My father's family, the McHargs, are all in Rangoon, my mother's are spread further afield in Taunggyi and Mandalay. These were the bad old days when tourists were allowed only a visa for a week in the country. I suppose I could have made a case for going in on compassionate grounds to see relatives, but this could have been risky. My mother, thirty years earlier, had been allowed only twenty-four hours to visit her dying mother. The official attitude to nationals who had left the country was unpredictable. Far better not to admit any Burmese connections at the outset and just organise my own independent itinerary when I arrived. My father's two youngest brothers, Peter and Jimmy, had emigrated to Australia. Auntie May, now a frail seventy-three-year-old widow, was living with the remaining brother, Johnny, in Botataung, a suburb of Rangoon. I asked my father about Johnny's family but he

wasn't forthcoming. He was never much of a letter writer
and had lost track of his Burmese nephews and nieces, being
more in touch with the Australian branch. However, he
wrote to Johnny, alerting him to my imminent arrival.

What should I take the family, I wondered. My father
said they were well off by Burmese standards, duty-free
cigarettes and whisky would be enough and maybe a copy
of the book I had just written. What about clothes for the
children? Surely even Burmese children would appreciate
T-shirts with pictures of red London buses? My father said
he didn't know what age or what size the children were.
Not to worry, we could send them on later. This was
optimistic. How much of the stuff my mother parcelled
up every Christmas for her relations in Taunggyi ever
reached its destination we never knew. By the time the
Customs workers and postmen had taken their share, my
other Auntie May, my mother's cousin and her family, were
lucky to salvage a couple of sweaters. We once sent them
a box of chocolates and heard afterwards that the box had
arrived plus all the little paper cups in which each chocolate
traditionally nestled but every last soft centre and hazelnut
whirl in both layers had been snaffled. You can just imagine
the family looking longingly at the key showing the different
fillings in each chocolate and rummaging hopefully through
the empty packaging.

No, that isn't true. I could imagine the empty box,
but I had no idea what May and her family looked like.
If I thought about it I dare say they would have fallen
somewhere between the beautiful kneeling Shan princess
over our fireplace and the huge, shapeless figure of Auntie
Dollie from my mother's teachers' training college dishing
out curry on Sunday afternoon in Wimbledon. I knew
they all wore Burmese dress and I could never fathom
how the Aran sweaters and Marks & Spencer cardigans
we sent would combine with the elegance of *longyis* and

lace blouses. 'It gets very cold in Taunggyi in the winter,' said my mother. After the war they had clothing coupons, just as we had in England, but they operated differently. You couldn't choose what you wanted with your coupons. You queued up and someone took your coupon and gave you whatever was available, a vest or a pair of socks. If they were too big or too small that was your bad luck. Under mother's direction I stocked up with winter woollies and a variety of chocolate and make-up, neither of which is available except at extortionate black-market prices in Burma.

The plan was to meet my friend Gaye in Bangkok and then proceed together into my land as my children insisted on calling it. I wish I could say I felt deep, grandiose feelings about going home, finding my true identity at last and all that sort of romantic twaddle, but I'm afraid I didn't. I was apprehensive, certainly, and curious but so was I whenever I travelled to unknown places. I also confess to feeling a bit worried in case my long-lost but soon to be found relatives turned out to be embarrassing. Would they spit like the Chinese I had just witnessed during the Royal Tour? The ravishingly beautiful receptionist in my hotel in Shanghai, a dead ringer for Madame Butterfly, exquisitely dressed and fluent in three languages, had suddenly turned her head sideways from the register she was writing in and shot a stream of spittle into the nearest potted palm.

My mother had warned me about going to visit her half-sister, Auntie Betty. Would I go on my own, she said and not take Gaye who might be appalled at the squalor. Of all my friends, the least likely to baulk at a little squalor was Gaye with whom two years previously I had survived being stranded for a week in the back of an Indian army convoy cut off by snow in Ladakh.

I had vague worries about not being able to communicate because, though my mother and stepfather spoke Burmese, they had never thought to teach me any. Quite the opposite.

They used it as a private language when they did not want my sister or me to understand what they were saying. It will be all right, reassured Gaye, as we joined the check-in line for Burma Air at Bangkok airport. You'll see, it will be wonderful. She was right.

The flight from Bangkok to Rangoon took less than two hours. In terms of quantum leaps and culture shocks it might have been two hundred years. Bangkok was everything that Rangoon was not, commercial, plastic, obsequious, Americanised, phoney. Rangoon is shabby, old-fashioned, creaking, where people stroll not bustle and there is all the time in the world to stop and talk and watch. In Bangkok there were two German back-packers checking in in front of us wearing thin cotton singlets and shorts. The Burma Air check-in girl looked at them for a long time. 'If you are going to Rangoon you will have to wear shirts, you cannot go like that,' she said. My mother had warned me about Burmese modesty. 'Don't take short skirts and see-through blouses,' she said. 'You will only embarrass people and make them think the less of you.' So we had carefully packed the sort of summer dresses we last wore at school prize giving, as well as sensible shoes for all the pagoda-crawling we intended to include in our visit.

It was odd landing at Rangoon. I didn't expect to see serried ranks of jumbo jets lined up on the tarmac but I had expected to see something. There was one small and not noticeably spruce military plane being worked on by mechanics as we landed. That was all. First impressions were rosy, literally deep pink, the earth, the hills receding in the distance, the roofs of the ramshackle buildings round the airport. There were people, lots of people, waving from the flat roof of the terminal as we walked across the tarmac and I was self-conscious that my relatives might be among them searching out the returning prodigal. We had been forewarned about Burmese Customs and Immigration.

You'll be there a couple of hours at least, they said, you'll fill in seventeen forms itemising every sock, hairpin and five-pence piece and you'll open and close your cases for inspection at least seventeen times. They were right but for some reason Gaye and I seemed to jump some of the queues and be hustled forward at others, our cases being less thoroughly scrutinised than those of our fellow passengers. It was as if someone had been told to look out for two unaccompanied ladies and give them a bit of a push. 'Do you have influential friends or something?' whispered Gaye as a Customs official put yet another chalk mark on our cases, indicating that it had passed yet another hurdle. I said doubtfully that Uncle Johnny was a grade two civil servant whatever that meant. It didn't sound as if it meant much.

We were at the last desk. The one where we declared what money we had. Not being mathematically inclined I had forgotten the other advice experienced travelling friends had given me about not declaring everything so that we could change money on the black market. Did we write down more or less than we had? When we came out in a week's time, and they checked our purchases and receipts, couldn't a discrepancy lead to trouble? I was scratching my head perplexedly when a pleasant male voice said, 'Hello, Susan. Had a good flight?' and I looked up to see my mother's old sweetheart turned diplomat, now retired, U Pe Kin, beside me.

I last saw him on a visit he and his wife made to the farm in Hampshire ten years ago. He hadn't changed, the same dapper figure dressed in beige linen slacks and elegant Nehru jacket. His English was flawless with only a slight and very attractive accent, the foreignness of it being more in the out-dated slang than anything else.

'Good heavens, it's Pe Kin,' I said, hugging him. 'Let me introduce my friend. How did you know we were here? Did my mother write? Where's Auntie Marjorie?'

I had better start calling him Uncle Pe Kin, because without the prefix it is as peremptory as calling him by his surname alone, as one addresses a manservant. I didn't appreciate this until a couple of days later when I had telephoned home and my mother, mortified, said would I please stop offending Pe Kin by treating him like the driver. It was her fault. She always referred to him as Pe Kin, just as she called my father McHarg.

Back at the airport Customs, Uncle Pe Kin looked hurt. 'Of course I knew all about your arrival. How do you suppose you got through so quickly? It is only because I have some influence over these people,' he said grandly. 'That is also why I have been allowed to pass through to this side. Please come this way, my driver is waiting outside and will take you to your hotel.'

Passing through to the Arrivals Lounge, I somehow became detached from Gaye and Uncle Pe Kin. At once I was surrounded by small surreptitious figures whispering, 'Would you like to change some money? Very good rate. Have you cigarettes? Have you whisky? A good price for Johnny Walker.'

'Please go away,' I said, 'I am looking for my uncle.'

'Over here, Susan, I am your uncle, your Uncle Maurice,' cried a voice I hadn't heard before and a dark, snake-like man with a huge purple wart on his eyelid pushed through the crowd towards me. Uncle Maurice? I didn't remember anything about an Uncle Maurice. I fished in my bag and got out my list of long-lost relatives – Auntie May, Uncle Jimmy, Uncle Johnny, Uncle Peter, Auntie Betty . . .

'There must be some mistake,' I said to the snake-like man with the purple wart. 'I haven't got an Uncle Maurice.'

'Yes, yes, Susan, I am the half-brother of your Uncle Johnny of Botataung. Your grandmother remarried Abdul Aziz, the taxi driver, in Maymyo and had three more children. I am the oldest of these,' he added with a certain pride. 'Now, come along and meet your Auntie and your cousins, they are all waiting for you.'

It was no good protesting. Uncle Maurice seized my elbow and steered me through the throng to some wooden benches in the centre of the hall where what looked like the entire cast of *The King and I* were assembled. There was a row of pretty giggling girls in rainbow-coloured *longyis*, behind them another row of serious and slightly shy-looking young men, while standing at the side like a caretaker, was a man who might have been my father's twin except that where my father was dark, this man was unnervingly pale, almost albino. He had his arm round a slight, elderly woman who had her fist pressed into her mouth and seemed to be overcome with emotion. Uncle Maurice did the honours. 'This is Susan. This is your Uncle Johnny' (pointing to the albino) 'and this is your Auntie Amah' (pointing to the lady with her fist in her mouth) 'and your cousins Irene, Olive, Kitty, Patricia . . .'

I sat down, it was all too much. When for thirty-odd years you have had but one mother, one father and one sister, the sudden addition of a legion of relatives can be an overwhelming experience. No wonder Auntie Amah looked dazed. It was much later I learned that Auntie Amah had been to the dentist that morning and had had all her teeth removed – the new ones weren't arriving until the following week. Uncle Johnny relieved Uncle Maurice as Master of Ceremonies. He gave brisk orders. 'George,' he said to one of the serious young men, 'take Susan's luggage to the car. The rest of you must come home by bus. Come along Susan, your Auntie May is at home waiting with presents and a meal.' It was at this point that Gaye and Uncle Pe Kin showed up and the trouble began.

How on earth both parties knew we were arriving on this plane, I never found out. We certainly hadn't alerted anyone but news travels fast among aunties and uncles in

Burma. However we played it, someone's nose was going to be put out of joint because both Uncle Johnny and Uncle Pe Kin were offering transport into town. Have I mentioned *arnadeh* already? It is one of those untranslatable Burmese words which roughly means exquisite politeness – an extreme consideration for other people's feelings so that nobody feels in any way put out, indebted or embarrassed. It was my duty now to display this. Clearly Uncle Pe Kin as the senior host – to say nothing of the fact that he was my mother's ex-boy-friend – had to be appeased. Both Uncles were looking askance at each other. I made the relevant introductions – they all murmured that they had indeed heard of the other and then I had a brainwave. 'Why don't we travel in convoy?' I suggested. 'I'll go in front with Uncle Pe Kin and Gaye can go with Uncle Johnny and take all those presents we brought.' This was a stroke of genius.

I have no wish to denigrate my long-lost relatives but they were pretty keen on presents. Gaye told me afterwards that Uncle Johnny had asked her how my book, *Little Princes*, had sold. I suppose my father must have written to tell them I had published a history of royal children earlier that year. Uncle Johnny took particular interest in the cover price of each book. He then multiplied this by five hundred and came to the conclusion I was very, very rich indeed. The cigarettes, the whisky, the chocolates and the make-up we had brought them failed by Uncle Johnny's calculations to reflect my newly acquired wealth. More on this later.

I don't remember how we disengaged ourselves from the retinue but somehow we found ourselves at the Strand Hotel in a room not unlike a youth hostel with summonses to attend Uncle Johnny's for dinner in Botataung at 7 p.m. and Uncle Pe Kin's for a buffet supper at 10 p.m. All we really wanted to do was sleep. It was incredibly hot. I found a plug for the bath, turned on the cold tap and a trickle of dark-brown water emerged. The bath didn't look as though it had been used since the Battle of Kohima. It was at this point that the heavens opened (I had forgotten it was the monsoon season). Streams of water started pouring through the ceiling. Gaye ran out into the passage to get help before our luggage floated away and found sundry hotel staff placing buckets, saucepans, large jars and any other suitable receptacle to hand at strategic intervals along the corridors. They were clearly used to this sort of emergency drill. My mother told me the Strand was the most fashionable hotel in the Far East when she was a girl. Alas, it wouldn't get a mention in the *AA Bed & Breakfast Guide* these days.

On to Botataung and a large, gloomy house in First Avenue where the rooms were puzzlingly uniform, part bedroom, part sitting-room, part stock-room. There were beds and sofas and boxes everywhere and big dark cupboards like the ones in the locker rooms at school. Uncle Johnny gave us a tour, talking non-stop about relatives I had never heard of, until at length we came to a small back room where Auntie May, my father's elder sister, was waiting to receive us. She was wrapped in so many shawls, I couldn't actually see her face but she did seem very, very old and wizened and her voice somewhere behind the veils was thin and small like an injured bird. 'How long I have waited for this moment, Susan. We have all been waiting for this moment. We know of your great success as a Royal Writer. Is it 500 books you have sold so far? You must have made a great deal of money.' This was the first of many references to my book sales which I am afraid to say were nowhere near their expectations. Last I saw of *Little Princes* was a huge cardboard box of remaindered copies on Waterloo station but the folks at home in Botataung weren't to know this.

Gaye was digging me in the ribs and whispering to me to look at the holy picture above Auntie May's bed. It was the famous Botticelli mother and child, which, whispered

Gaye, was exactly the same as the one she had at school at Elmhurst, remember? Why hadn't I told her Auntie May was a Roman Catholic? Because I didn't know it myself, for heaven's sake, I returned savagely. I thought they were all Buddhists.

Even as we spoke, Uncle Johnny was telling us about Cousin Frank who had become a *phongyi* at the monastery in Sagaing. This was thrilling news. On the plane coming out Gaye had furnished me with reading material about Burma and I had been fascinated by the accounts of *phongyis* and monasteries. Buddhist monks, I read, are allowed but five earthly possessions: saffron robe, sandals, begging bowl, sun umbrella and fan. Now I had a cousin with a begging bowl and a saffron robe. This was something to regale those Fleet Street hacks with at the Albion at lunch-times. If only he had been called something a little more exotic than Frank.

We had dinner in what I took to be the front parlour, more beds, sofas and boxes and a low table spread with curry and rice. When I say 'we', I exclude all the females of the household apart from Gaye and myself. This seemed to be the way they did it at Uncle Johnny's. He sat pale and aloof at the head of the table, Gaye and I on either side, and the shy, serious boy cousins taking up the rest of the places, while at the back, behind the sort of bead curtain you see in hairdressers in Kenton, the distaff side of the household peeked and giggled and chattered as we ate. It was all a bit unnerving, particularly when with a rattle and a screech of tyres an extraordinary little cart trundled into the room driven by a smiling lad who seemed to be all head and whirring arms and nothing much below the waist. First impressions proved correct. This was Nicky, my nephew, a polio victim with wasted nether limbs for whom Uncle Maurice had built this ingenious contraption in lieu of a wheelchair. Wheelchairs are hard to come by in Burma. With admirable dexterity, Nicky manoeuvred his go-kart round the sofas, beds and boxes and came to a halt in front of me. 'Greetings, Auntie Sue,' he cried and then as far as I could make out, he repeated TV, TV, TV, TV, over and over again. I glanced at Gaye. She looked apprehensive. I looked to Uncle Johnny for an explanation. He was steadily tucking into prawn crackers and rice but raised his head briefly to explain that my nephew was very fond of television and had hoped that I might have bought him a set with all the money I had earned from the sale of my book.

We talked about my father, we talked about my sister and her children and, I suppose, other items of family interest but all I could really think about was the ghoulish figure of Nicky at my knee. Whenever I caught his eye, which I tried very hard to avoid doing, his grin would stretch from ear to ear and he would again gabble TV, TV, TV. Had he been eleven years old, I might have excused it, but it turned out that Nicky was twenty-two, married, with three small children. Maybe I am being uncharitable. Maybe he was pleading on behalf of his family. We handed over our Marlboro cigarettes and Scotch whisky and in return were given woven shoulder bags, garishly coloured table cloths and silk *longyis* to take home to my sister.

In the background I could hear someone singing, 'Little Jesus, sweetly sleep, do not stir, We will lend a coat of fur.' Surely not my Auntie May, the voice sounded much younger. No, said my Uncle Johnny, it was the Karen girl who helped out in the kitchen. Karens were Christians. This one had been converted to Catholicism by Auntie May. I vaguely knew about the Karens from my father. He referred to them as insurgents. You couldn't travel independently in Burma he told me, because of the insurgents, i.e. the Karens who occupied the middle section of Burma between Rangoon and Taunggyi. Only the month before, Uncle Maurice explained, a brigade of soldiers had kidnapped all the wives from a Karen village and held them hostage.

What happened? I enquired breathlessly – it sounded like an Alistair MacLean adventure story. The following week, the Karens kidnapped the soldiers' wives, replied Uncle Johnny laconically still working his way through prawn crackers and rice.

All through the meal, above the sound of the giggling girls behind the bead curtain and the squeaking of Nicky's go-kart, I could hear a continual pounding coming from a back room. 'What is it?' I asked George. 'They are making *balachan*,' he said. Ah, so that was it. I knew all about *balachan* from my mother who bought jars of the stuff every time we went to places like Southall which had ethnic food stores. *Balachan* is a pickle as popular in Burma as HP Sauce in England. It is a pungent mixture of dried prawns, garlic and fish paste which smells unambiguously of drains. When we left Botataung, Auntie May pressed a bottle of *balachan* into both Gaye's hands and mine.

I wish I could have warmed to my Uncle Johnny a little more but there was something sinister about his pale skin, white hair and pinkish eyes. That, together with his constant reference to how much more money we had in England than their family had ever had in Burma, made it difficult to get past the polite stage of a relationship and, in the end, I limited my conversation to questions about his childhood with my father. He didn't tell me much more than I already knew. He had gone to the university and become what he ingenuously called a 'Second Grade Civil Servant' working for the Customs and Excise Department. It didn't sound exactly strenuous. Uncle Johnny drove us in his forty-year-old Austin to York Avenue, the well-heeled suburb where Uncle Pe Kin and his wife Marjorie lived. Yes, of course, we said, we would visit him again before we left for London but we knew we wouldn't.

U Pe Kin's residence was a Burmese's idea of an elegant English-style home; where Uncle Johnny's was overcrowded, Uncle Pe Kin's was sparse to the point of austerity. The drawing-room had twelve high-backed mahogany chairs placed formally against the walls like a doctor's waiting-room. They were very uncomfortable but we perched on them for an hour drinking sherry from ornate, pink-stemmed glasses while Uncle Pe Kin told us about his diplomatic postings in Moscow, Cairo and Washington. Auntie Marjorie, who had the same regal bearing and bosom as Dame Edith Evans, whittered on about how difficult it was to find good domestic servants these days. Rangoon, in some aspects, isn't so different from Reigate. The pride of Uncle Pe Kin's foreign travel was his dining-room table which could seat twenty-four and had a simulated teak/formica top. It didn't strike him as remotely odd that anyone would prefer simulated teak to the real thing – teak along with rubies is Burma's major asset – but Auntie Marjorie was clearly enchanted with its easy-wipe surface. She wiped it with a cloth every time a new dish was served.

Uncle Pe Kin is a very un-Burmese Burmese. For a start he is a Moslem which raises a few difficulties. Moslems are not allowed to run businesses in Burma (or at least they weren't at that time) so his two sons Ko Ko and Nyi Nyi – translating literally as big brother and small brother – were having to work in neighbouring Malaysia. They were both doing hotel management courses. I remember Nyi Nyi coming to stay with us at North Lodge when he was ten years old. He had been sent to some posh prep school in Surrey and Uncle Pe Kin had asked my mother to take care of him during one Easter holidays. They took their religion extremely seriously. One night my mother heard a noise in the kitchen, tiptoed downstairs and found ten-year-old Nyi Nyi peering into the fridge. 'What on earth are you doing, Nyi Nyi, it is 2 in the morning. Are you hungry?' No he wasn't. He was just checking to see that the bacon in the fridge was nowhere near any of the other food that he might have to eat.

Having spent his entire professional life in Government service, it wasn't surprising to hear Uncle Pe Kin defending the dreaded General Ne Win, unenlightened despot of Burma for the last thirty-odd years. It was no good asking Uncle Pe Kin about the crateloads of rubies and jade disappearing into numbered accounts in Switzerland. Uncle said he knew nothing of these wicked rumours. Ne Win had a difficult row to hoe (U Pe Kin had picked up some quaint slang in his years abroad) and was doing a tolerably good job. He could forgive him anything, he said, because he was a very fine golfer. Many is the afternoon my uncle and the General had passed together on the golf course near the Inya Lake.

There would be time enough to hear the other side of the story of the everyday life of Burmese folk. Next morning we were due to visit Auntie Betty and her husband U Sein Koh in their down-at-heel quarter of Rangoon. We planned to have lunch with them on our way to the airport to fly up-country. Having only seven days meant these family reunions were having to be achieved at high speed. Well, at least it meant only one night at the Strand Hotel. What a mausoleum, what a dump. You could see it had known glory days. There were wide marble staircases and banqueting rooms with domed ceilings but now all you could see were the saucepans spread out like croquet hoops to catch the monsoon downpour.

Auntie Betty lived in Molet Saung Gong, the Rangoon equivalent to the Balls Pond Road. We had some difficulty finding a taxi driver to take us. This was unnerving, was it a no-go area? Nor did there seem to be a proper address. My mother had written the directions in Burmese on an envelope which I flashed at the cab driver, even so it took many stops and starts and arm-waving and shouting before we eventually pulled up on a dirt track in a setting which might have graced the cover of *National Geographic Magazine*. This was light-years from anything I had ever visited in my life before and I prided myself on being well-travelled and unshockable. To Gaye, used to the obsessive hygiene of an Austrian mother-in-law's household, it must have been something of a culture shock too.

Everything seemed to be happening in the street, there were people squatting, sitting, cooking, washing, sleeping, reading, fighting and as far as I could see, giving birth and dying as well. Our taxi caused a tremendous stir. As soon as it stopped it was surrounded by children attempting to swarm through the windows, climb on to the bonnet, or pull themselves up on to the roof. The taxi driver swatted them away like flies but it was impossible, there were far too many.

'Where is Daw Sein Ohn?' I asked, using Auntie Betty's Burmese name. At once a dozen willing guides showed us the way, grabbing our hands, pulling at our skirts. They directed us to a rickety wooden house, three storeys high with an outside staircase and a great deal of washing flapping from the balconies. Up the stairs we went to another of those multi-purpose bedroom-parlour-storage units. This one had an extraordinary collection of chairs, old padded armchairs bursting at the seams, wooden kitchen chairs, canvas deck-chairs, stools, cushions. It could easily have accommodated thirty sitting people but there was only one person in sight, a young girl bending over what looked like a bundle of old clothes that turned out to be a very small baby.

Our small guides had accompanied us and were now all talking at once pointing to us, pointing to the taxi driver, pointing to the young girl who looked bemused and then twigged. She ran into a back room and seconds later a small, tousled man in vest and *longyi* came out, rubbing his eyes as if he had just woken up. To me he looked as foreign as a Tuareg or an Inca.

'You are Marjorie's daughter. I am Uncle Sein Koh,' he said. 'Please sit. We will fetch your Auntie Betty. She is at the pagoda. We have all been waiting for you.'

At some stage one of the small boys is despatched to the pagoda and in the meantime Gaye and I are offered refreshment. Some of the less exotic chairs are offered and as we eat gram crackers with strange hot dips, Uncle Sein Koh shows us a dog-eared photograph album. For the first time, I see a photograph of my grandmother, Daw Shweh Ohn, my mother's mother, the one who was given an elephant in lieu of money. She must have been about fifty when it was taken. She is sitting on a rock looking unnervingly like Queen Victoria – not at all amused. I try to remember those stories my mother told about swatting mosquitoes with her cheroot while regaling her with the history of the Burmese Kings and Queens, but it is difficult to equate that fierce little figure with such romance. No sign of Auntie Betty. Maybe we should go to the pagoda and meet her, suggests Uncle Sein Koh. So down we all go and by the time we get to the street, I am feeling like the Pied Piper with a procession of children in tow – not exactly dancing and singing, Burmese children are well-behaved, but clearly having a good time.

That morning at dawn, we had visited the famous Shwedagon Pagoda in the centre of the city, so we are now used to the whole business of Buddhist ceremonies. We were instructed to buy flowers at the entrance and strew them over the temple dedicated to our particular birth date. Mine is Wednesday and represented by a mythical figure called a Chintheh – part dragon, part horse. After this, you perform the ceremony known as washing and wishing. This involves simply dunking yourself with a bucket of cold water and praying that in your next reincarnation you will be something a little more elevated than a beetle. It was hardly the sort of ambience you associate with religious pilgrimage, nothing like the hushed interior of St Peter's, or the vast emptiness of St Sofia. As usual there were crowds of people, whole families washing and wishing, strewing and chatting and eating their lunch – and, of course, taking photographs. A visit to the Shwedagon is the Burmese equivalent to a day out in London watching the Changing of the Guards.

The pagoda at Molet Saung Gong is less lavish. It looked more like a half-finished garage with just its roof and no walls. People were strolling in and out like shoppers – Buddhism seems a very casual sort of religion. Going to the pagoda is as ordinary as going to Sainsbury's. At one end of the building was the ubiquitous Buddha figure wreathed in flowers with candles round it and in the main body of the wall-less space people were kneeling, sitting or lying full-length on straw mats moving their lips in silent prayer. Others stood chanting monotonously as I had seen the monks doing in Ladakh three years earlier on that ill-fated trip to India.

'There she is,' said Uncle Sein Koh and pointed to a slight figure in a spotless white blouse and royal-blue *longyi*. Was this really Auntie Betty of whom my mother had spoken so emotionally for all these years? Auntie Betty with the very dark skin whose father (my mother's stepfather Ko Ko) had almost certainly had dog-Indian blood?

The figure that rose from its kneeling position was certainly dark, it also had the saddest face I have ever seen. Auntie Betty had been prostrating herself like a Moslem facing Mecca on a prayer mat, her forehead on a narrow wooden block which she now picked up, carefully dusted down and tucked under her arm. This was my first encounter with Buddhist prayer rests. Auntie Betty had every reason to look sad – her oldest son was in prison for drug-dealing and before that he had ruined the family by stealing all Auntie Betty's savings. What savings, I asked my mother when she was telling me the sorry saga. The idea of Auntie Betty having a nest-egg at the Rangoon branch of TSB was absurd. My mother explained.

When my grandmother died, she had left what jewels she still possessed to Auntie Betty. Had she been able to, she would have divided them equally between Betty and my mother but it was impossible to send jewellery out of the country, so Betty had got it all. My mother could describe every item of this fabulous legacy in detail, every bracelet, necklace and brooch, including the number of stones and how big they all were. Betty had kept these in an iron chest under her bed and whenever the family needed money she would sell a piece. And then one day, the good-for-nothing oldest son stole the box and sold the contents to feed his habit. At a stroke the family was reduced to penury and the ramshackle tenement in Molet Saung Gong. It all seemed a bit far-fetched, especially the description of the jewels compared to which the contents of Aladdin's cave were but an item in the Argos catalogue. I have always said my mother exaggerated and then she too went to Burma to see her sister and came back with one of Betty's last remaining brooches which took my breath away. It was the size of a coffee saucer, an exquisite replica of a fern made of gold and studded with rubies. She had to hide it from the Customs in the toe of her shoe, as it is illegal to take rubies out of Burma for anyone but General Ne Win. The gold was so pure and so very soft that even this brief period of concealment had bent the brooch out of shape.

Auntie Betty taught English at the local High School, her own was flawless and almost without accent. Not that she spoke much, she was crying too hard; she just kept hugging me and saying 'How is Marjorie? How is Marjorie?' This was all too much for Gaye and me. I am easily given to tears. When I tell the children bedtime stories, I can work myself into such an emotional state that by the time Little

Red Riding Hood has got to Grandmother's cottage, I am snivelling so hard I cannot finish the story. So we stood there in the pagoda, Auntie Betty, Gaye and I, blubbing copiously while unknown relatives and sundry spectators watched in polite silence. They made no attempt to cheer us up. Uncle Sein Koh asked if I had caught a chill, I think he thought I was sneezing. Back at the house, we looked again at the photograph album and talked about how pretty my mother was fifty years ago and then it was time for us to go on to the airport for our flight to Heho, the airport for Taunggyi, the next stop on our itinerary. We had asked the taxi to wait. Auntie Betty insisted on coming with us, even though she had no official pass to get into the airport. In Burma, airports are restricted places. You can't just walk in and out of them, you have to apply for a pass in advance to meet or deliver a passenger. 'But what will you do, Auntie, if you can't come in with us? No, honestly, don't come, we will see you when we return to Rangoon next week,' I said, but Auntie Betty was adamant. So were her children who followed in a ramshackle vehicle borrowed from a friend and thus in convoy once more we proceeded to Rangoon airport.

Hang on, wasn't there someone missing? Where was Susan, my cousin, Auntie Betty's oldest daughter? My mother had always wanted Susan to come to England to stay with us, to give her a chance in life, which meant marrying an Englishman. Susan had become a nun for six months which was why she was not present at this poignant family reunion, said Auntie Betty. I didn't know you could be a nun for six months, wasn't it a life-time vocation? Auntie Betty explained the circumstances. Susan had just finished three years reading Physics and Chemistry at Rangoon University and was studying for her Finals. It was hard work but she had had the sense to make a deal with her *nyat* that if she passed, she would dedicate six months of her life to prayer. Her exam results were better than anyone expected and accordingly she had taken herself off to the local *phongyi*, had all her hair shaved, put on a saffron robe and was probably at this very moment doing the rounds of the houses with her begging bowl. 'You will see her when you come back from Taunggyi,' promised Auntie Betty. 'I will make sure she has permission to visit us.' I wanted to ask Auntie Betty if this sort of academic bargain was the norm among students but it seemed impolite. I was getting the hang of *arnadeh* already.

There was a pitiful moment outside the airport, where, despite my pleading, the security guard refused to allow Auntie Betty to come in. The Burmese are extraordinarily schizophrenic. In *longyis* and sandals they are the most gentle, accommodating people. Put them in a uniform and heavy-duty laced-up boots and they become Tartars. Useless me beseeching that this was my long-lost auntie whom I had never seen in thirty-odd years and might never see again. 'Where is your official permit? No admittance without an official permit,' he repeated. So once more we hugged and sobbed and vowed to see each other in a week and then Gaye and I passed through to the Departure Lounge where – oh horrors – I recognised the familiar screech of go-kart wheels and there were the Clan Johnny from First Avenue, Botataung, including the grinning Nicky, who *had* had the foresight to procure official permits and had come to see us off. There was no escaping. Uncle Johnny, palely sinister, was holding the copy of *Little Princes* I had given him as a present and was telling the girl behind the Burma Air desk how many copies I had sold and what a very rich woman I was. 'TV, Auntie Sue, TV,' repeated Nicky, trundling furiously around my knees. We had hoped to spend a little time before the flight in the gift shop but with this crowd around us we decided to go straight through Customs. Gaye was tactful. All she said was that Nicky might not be quite as enthusiastic about getting a TV if he saw some of the programmes on offer. My lasting memory of walking across the tarmac to the plane is of Uncle Johnny et al. waving energetically from the roof of the airport building and like the Mock Turtle's 'soup of the evening, beautiful soup' the strains of Nicky's 'TV, Auntie Sue, TV' faded into the afternoon haze.

Air travel has never been my forte. The more flights I take, the more terrified I am, so much so that I once took a British Airways course for nervous fliers. This involved a day spent in a simulator pretending to be the pilot of a jumbo jet landing in New York. The Manhattan skyline reared up at me through the windscreen and one by one my engines failed but thanks to the efficacy of modern technology (and of course my aviatory expertise) we landed perfectly safely on one engine. How this was supposed to make me feel confident about flying, God only knows. I emerged from my simulated 747 Boeing jumbo jet a quivering heap, determined never to set foot on an aircraft again. Some hope. Still, with a good book and some loud earphones I usually manage to stave off the impulse to shriek every time I take off or land, but that flight from Rangoon to Heho was a stern test of the equilibrium. Neither of our safety belts functioned and the panel beside the window was hanging loose. When I opened the overhead locker to put in my travelling case, the door came off in my hands. As for the flight itself, we were buffeted around for an hour like tickets in a tombola, ducking and diving through turbulence with never a word to soothe or comfort over the intercom. 'I think we are there,' said Gaye, who was sitting by the window. She is built of sterner stuff than me and had been looking out over the miniature landscape. 'Oh, no, maybe not, unless we are landing in a field with a garden shed at the bottom.'

That is precisely what we were doing. Heho airport is the size of your average London school playing-field and the terminal not much larger than your average allotment shack. At this moment I wouldn't have cared had we been landing on the side of the Eiger, I just wanted to be out of that lethal machine. Only four of us were disembarking. Burma Air has an idiosyncratic scheduling system. There are only two flights a day from Rangoon, both circular, one going clockwise the other anti-clockwise; we were on the second, that is, Rangoon, Heho, Mandalay, Pagan, Rangoon. Independent passengers, as we were (travelling without a group or on business), ran the risk of being bumped if the flight was overbooked. It invariably was and only a large bribe could get you a seat. We had become used to dishing out bribes in the two days we had been in Burma.

It took a little time to extract our luggage from the bowels of the plane. We had with us one enormous suitcase full of thick sweaters, thermal vests and blankets for Auntie May, courtesy of my mother. In amongst the folds of clothing were giant bars of Cadbury's Whole Nut Chocolate and tins of Quality Street and Roses which the avaricious fingers of the Customs department had overlooked and some freckle-removal cream my aunt had specifically asked for, much to my mother's amusement. The method of locating our luggage was simple, if slow. Every last suitcase belonging to the sixty or so passengers was taken out and lined up on the runway; we then identified ours, checked the labels against our passports and staggered into the garden shed with them. There were no porters or trolleys, playing-fields don't provide such luxuries.

Surely, this being an internal flight, we would not have to go through that tiresome rigmarole of Customs declarations again? I was about to say that we were only visiting a relative when the clerk, who had been busily writing in a ledger said, 'Yes, I know. You are going to stay with your Auntie May in Theik-Pan Road.' Good grief! This wasn't another hitherto unknown relative like Uncle Maurice, was it?

'How on earth do you know about my Auntie May?' I said, faintly.

'Everyone knows you are coming to see Auntie May,' said the clerk in a matter-of-fact tone and there the matter appeared to rest.

'Well, if you know so much about my affairs,' I snapped, 'perhaps you could let me know what arrangements have been made for us to reach Taunggyi.'

'Certainly, there is a jeep with a driver waiting outside to take you to the Taunggyi Hotel,' he said, without looking up.

In normal circumstances the drive to Taunggyi takes two hours. These were not normal circumstances. At what stage we discovered we did not have Auntie May's suitcase full of sweaters and Quality Street in the back of the jeep I cannot say. All I remember is Gaye giving a little shriek and saying, 'Oh, my God! What happened to the suitcase?' and the driver stamping on the brakes and the pair of us rummaging hopelessly in the back to no avail. We must have left it behind in the garden shed. There was no question of arriving without it, if Auntie May was one tenth as eager for her presents as Uncle Johnny and Co. had been, giftless our reception would be frosty indeed.

We returned to Heho. The clerk was still writing in the ledger. There was no one else to approach, so we approached him. Again, without looking up, 'The big blue suitcase with the two red labels was put on the truck for the Inle Lake Hotel,' he said. 'You will have to collect it from there. It is not too far out of your way.' I remembered the Inle Lake Hotel truck; the other two passengers who had disembarked with us, a German couple, were spending two nights there. Our luggage must have been mistaken for theirs. Oh well, at least we might get a chance to see the famous leg-rowers mentioned in every guidebook.

We didn't see the leg-rowers, we saw something far

more spectacular. Turning a dusty corner some twenty miles from Heho on the road to the lake, we suddenly drive slap into a fairy-tale. A long procession of ponies, gorgeously apparelled, is coming towards us. On each sits a small boy dressed like a king. They wear golden crowns, gold stars are painted on their faces, their costumes are heavy with flowers and jewels and bells, and beside each walks an adult attendant holding a lacquer umbrella over the potted potentate's head. What on earth – of course, it is a *shin-pyu*, the Buddhist equivalent of a first communion. For three months the child will live like a real *phongyi* – shaved head, orange robe, begging bowl.

Behind the ponies comes a lorry so crowded with people that the vehicle is invisible. A small space has been cleared on the back and a *pwe* is in full tilt. Literally, a *pwe* is a demonstration of Burmese dancing. The reality is impossible to describe. In Bangkok we saw classical Thai dancers in stiff, elaborate costumes moving so delicately, so woodenly. The dancer on the back of the truck is not wood, she is fire – a child of about ten with a mane of tangled hair and a small, glowing face. Like quicksilver she leaps, arches, pirouettes, her palms stretched back towards her wrists like soaring birds, her feet tossing up the hem of her *longyi* like flames licking round dry logs. It is magic, pure magic. We stand by the roadside – villagers, children, chickens, dogs and two large black pigs. At last, ponies and *pwe* disappear round the corner and we return to our jeep. It seems very quiet, very empty and a little sad.

7

Auntie May and Aye-Aye-Moh

The Taunggyi Hotel where we have booked to stay three nights is on the outskirts of the town. It has taken all afternoon to get here thanks to the *pwe* and the detour to the Inle Lake Hotel (no leg-rowers, they had packed it in by the time we got there). We turn into a drive lush with jungle foliage, huge red blossoms the size and shape of chandeliers brush the roof of the jeep and suddenly we are skirting a large, formal lawn and rose garden where a wedding reception is in full swing. We learn afterwards that it started after lunch but Burmese weddings are long-drawn-out affairs, full of formal speeches and toasts, not so different from ours, and now the dancing was underway. Even so, the guests break off to stare as we climb, dusty and dishevelled, from the jeep and lug Auntie May's wretched suitcase behind us into the lobby. This time we affect no surprise whatsoever when the receptionist tells us that Auntie May has already telephoned and been alerted to the reason for our delay ('She is very pleased you found her suitcase,' adds the receptionist) and will be with us at 8 p.m. It is now 7 p.m. What we should really like is a large stiff gin, a cold bath and a couple of hours' sleep in a darkened room with cucumber slices over our eyes but there is no time for trifles. My mother swore me to look my very, very best for Auntie May. The reputation of the family was at stake, so please would I make sure to have clean hair, lipstick and a freshly ironed dress for the occasion. 'You have the gin,' I said to Gaye. 'I have got to get ready.'

When at eight o'clock I walk into the lobby and see Auntie May it is like seeing my mother in Burmese dress. It isn't just that she speaks perfect English (for forty years she has taught English in the front room of her house); her whole demeanour, her carriage, her air are European. Those English missionaries who taught my mother and her cousin certainly did a thorough job.

We order tea and immediately Auntie May starts firing a lifetime's worth of questions like a succession of darts. How old are my children, how many are at school, are they clever, how is my sister, when is her baby due? She sits next to me, so alert, so impatient, so un-Burmese. In her pale *longyi* and a thick Aran cardigan (sent by my mother years ago), her tiny hands clasped in her lap, she could easily be one of those delicate ivory statuettes.

'I would like to see your mummy again. Is she well?'

'She's fine. When did you last see her?'

Auntie May was vague. They had never become close as children. The age difference of four years was probably just too great, and in adolescence they had drifted apart. Auntie May was in Mawchi when my grandmother made it back home minus her motor car. 'Your grandmother was weeping. "Where is Marjorie?" I asked her. "She has gone to Mandalay with the other officers' wives, she has taken the baby," said your grandmother. And then your mummy did the trek to India with your sister and I never saw her again. Tell me, is she still so pretty?'

We make plans. In the morning, says Auntie May, we

must go round to her humble house and meet the rest of the family. Her eldest daughter Marjorie is married to a schoolteacher called Peter. (I am getting terribly confused with all these Mays and Marjories – was there a film star called Marjorie after whom everybody named their child?) They have two children, a daughter, (Aye-Aye-Moh) studying mathematics at Mandalay University and a younger boy, Toto. There are other children, Winston and David, and a colony of cousins who all appear to be living in the same house but no doubt I shall be making head and tail of this seemingly endless litany of relatives in the morning. When she leaves at last Gaye says, 'I can just imagine her teaching all her schoolchildren Christmas carols – she is very bossy but I like her.'

I did, too, though with feelings of guilt, because I know my mother's relationship with May was complex. She didn't seem to like May. Whether she too was feeling guilty because she had abandoned ship so to speak and made her life in England, leaving May to take care of her mother, I cannot say. Certainly all I ever heard my mother say about her was critical. She was grasping, she was jealous, she was a total spendthrift. How a shopaholic could go wild in Taunggyi, I could not imagine. 'Oh, jewels, of course,' said my mother. 'All Burmese women want jewels and more jewels.' Auntie May had not been wearing any jewels, not even the plainest pearl ear-rings. The most damning thing my mother said of her cousin was that she gambled heavily, playing Mah-jong every night in the Chinese Quarter and losing all the house-keeping money. If this was true, I wanted to see it. Maybe next day, we could arrange a trip to the Casino.

By comparison to poor Auntie Betty's set-up, Auntie May's house was in deepest middle-class suburbia. The houses were wooden bungalows with verandahs round them and all sorts of annexes hitched on to the back like a succession of sheds. Burmese families, I was learning, are nothing if not extended; these sheds were the bedroom annexes for the hangers-on. We were not invited to look round the residence. Our visit was confined to the large living-room which doubled as a schoolroom in term-time. It was now the summer vacation. On the back wall there hung a large blackboard on which someone had written in beautifully neat white-chalk handwriting *Auntie Sue, Welcome To Our Humble Home*. It was all a little embarrassing but not half as embarrassing as the inspection of the troops that I was now being invited to undertake.

There must have been sixteen people lined up in front of the blackboard standing in the 'at ease' military position, feet slightly apart, hands clasped Duke of Edinburgh style behind back, chins up and eyes staring straight ahead. No one smiled until Auntie May said, 'Everyone this is Auntie Sue and her friend Gaye from England.' At which point, sixteen pairs of eyes turned in our direction and sixteen voices intoned 'Welcome Auntie Sue'.

One by one I shook hands with children who came up to my knee and men who towered over me, forgetting each name as soon as it was replaced by another. My cousin, Marjorie, a woman approaching forty, pointed out the family photographs of my sister graduating from St Andrews University and asked how her job at the hospital was going. 'How do you know all about Jenny's work?' I asked Marjorie. She said they had scrap-books in which all the major events of our lives were recorded. They probably knew more about my sister's career than I did. That I knew nothing about their lives did not strike them in any way as odd, unless they were observing *arnadeh*. It wasn't my fault, this ignorance, I told myself. It was my mother's. Why had she not kept me in touch with all these people, why had we not had a scrap-book with pictures of Winston and Toto and Aye-Aye-Moh? I knew why. It was my mother denying those origins of hers, the same as I had been denying mine to the woman buying napkins in the General Trading Company. She was finished with all those dark-skinned people that were holding her back from the life she felt she was entitled to. The less we knew about Toto and Aye-Aye-Moh the better was my mother's attitude.

With an imperious gesture of her tiny hand, Auntie May cleared the room of all the company except Marjorie whose duty from now on was to act as punkah-wallah. It had grown very hot. Marjorie stood behind the stools on which we were now sitting with a large palm leaf, waving it gently backwards and forwards to create a cooling draught. It sounds rather dreadful writing it in cold print, as if Gaye and I were visiting potentates with a servant to do our bidding, but somehow it did not feel that way. Marjorie was in no way subservient. She just waved her palm, smiling serenely as if it were the most natural thing in the world to be given the role of a human air-conditioner. We talked more about the family at home in England.

Auntie May wanted to know everything about the farm, how many tractors had we owned, how many pigs, how many farm-hands? She seemed to think we had the equivalent of an estate in Sutherland, not a smallholding with one pigman, formerly a taxi driver at Liphook station. It occurred to me later that my mother may have exaggerated the picture, quadrupled the acreage, added gillies, stalkers, farm managers, dairy maids and heaven knows what manner of diverse livestock. And I was now spilling the beans and landing my mother right in it, but I didn't care. The time had come to tell it like it really was. I did not mince words about the farm going bankrupt either. I positively wallowed in the description of our newly reduced circumstances with my stepfather running a country post office and my mother trying to sell ethnic bric-à-brac in one corner of the shop. I am not sure Auntie May appreciated the finer nuances of our plunge from high-life in Hampshire to shop-keeping in Buckinghamshire, but her sharp little eyes were fixed unblinkingly on my face throughout.

'And tell me, Susan,' she said, 'what does your husband do?'

'He is a stockbroker.'

'What is a stockbroker?'

'Well, he takes other people's money and puts it in stocks and shares, to make it grow into more money,' I said, struggling with what to me too is a pretty esoteric art. 'He tries to make people richer.'

Auntie May leans forward, her eyes wide. 'Is that legal?' she says.

We have finished our mid-morning tea. It is time, says Auntie May, to visit the market where she will personally buy us Shan bags which are as ubiquitous in Burma as wooden clogs in Holland or flamenco dollies in Spain. But these would be the genuine article, because we were in the Southern Shan States where the bags were used as genuine containers, not tourist trinkets.

Going to market with her is like going on a magical mystery tour. Women from the hill villages sit on the ground in front of huge baskets overflowing with – with what? Heaven knows what those strange mud-coloured cakes are, or those long fronded vegetables or those tiny brick-coloured beans. I've never seen so many kinds of bean. Auntie May talks all the time. We have to stop at every stall and tell every stall-holder that I am her niece visiting from London, that I am married to a stockbroker who does queer things with other people's money. I am not sure how much of this gets through to the stall-holders but they smile and point at my watch and ask many, many questions to which Auntie May always has a ready reply.

And then something extraordinary happens. We have come to a stall where all that appears to be on sale are three flat brown cakes like old griddle scones. There is an ancient toothless woman sitting cross-legged on the mud floor behind the counter smoking a cheroot with an extraordinarily complex arrangement of scarves piled high on her head like a double-decker turban. This, explains Auntie May, is a typical Shan peasant's head-dress. The woman comes to market every week from her home in the hills and then the ancient toothless woman says something and Auntie May becomes excited. She starts chattering and nodding her head and points at me; she then says that the woman remembers my mother. I look just like her. She has been coming to the market for sixty years and used to sell cakes to my grandmother and her children.

For the first time since arriving in Burma I feel a genuine link with my roots. The relatives didn't seem to count. They were bound, all of them (Betty, May, Pe Kin) to know about our family and its history but here was a complete stranger who had actually recognised me because of my likeness to a woman she hadn't seen for half a century. I ask Auntie May to ask the woman what she remembers of my mother. No, I don't want to hear that she was pretty. I am fed up with hearing how pretty she was. I want to know what she said, what she did, whether any inkling of those deep-rooted ambitions of hers was evident all those years ago. All I get is that my mother was a happy little girl, always chattering, always busy and of course, very, very, pretty. Oh well, it was worth trying. I am not sure how my mother will relish hearing of this incident. It is not the sort of story she would have entertained those friends of hers in Hampshire with unless she could have moved the goal-posts just a fraction and made the toothless hag into a Shan princess.

But Auntie May has other plans. She has arranged for a very good friend of hers called Myint whose husband owns a tobacco factory to take us for a drive in Myint's motor car. Auntie May always calls them motor cars. 'Myint has a very grand house,' says Auntie May. 'Her husband is very rich. She has everything she wants – by the way, did you get that freckle cream I wrote to your mother about? It was for Myint.' Ah, so that was the mystery of the freckle cream. We had had this long, involved letter concerning a special form of skin treatment which somehow contrived to lighten freckles. Auntie May had provided a brand name which, needless to say, proved impossible to find. Numerous enquiries at dispensing chemists had eventually succeeded in producing a tube of something called Freckle Bleach. The chemist and I had agreed that freckles were attractive features and should be left well alone but there was no accounting for taste.

Fully expecting to see an older oriental version of Violet Elizabeth Bott, I was surprised to find Myint as lovely as the Shan princess in my mother's picture. Not a freckle in sight. She greeted us at the door of a long, cool room on an upper floor. There were shutters over the windows which made the interior too dim to make out anything but dark shapes of carved cupboards and rattan *chaises longues*. It was all very elegant, no wonder Auntie May was impressed. Myint was fully acquainted with all the details of our family, Auntie May had prepared her in advance, so the conversation moved smoothly enough and I felt sufficiently at ease to ask why she wanted freckle cream. She didn't have any freckles. Myint blushed. 'It is not really for my freckles,' she confessed. 'I rub it all over my face to make it paler. My husband prefers light skin.'

As if waiting for his cue, we heard footsteps and her husband arrived to take us on the promised motor tour. He was a small, round, jolly man who spoke no English but laughed a lot. I should have liked to ask him if he honestly thought a tube of freckle cream would make his wife more attractive but we had reached his tobacco factory, our first port of call, and anyway it would have been too difficult to explain my curiosity.

In a large, airy room, girls were sitting cross-legged on the ground, sorting cheroot-wrapping leaves in sizes as if they were dealing a hand of poker. It had nothing of the assembly-line atmosphere you associate with factories. It looked fun and the girls were chatting and laughing as they worked. They took no interest whatsoever in us. We drove round Taunggyi. Auntie May pointed out the Anglican church where now only she and the attendant priest are regular communicants. She pointed out the new hospital and the Chinese Quarter where presumably she whiled away her nights playing Mah-jong and then we were back in the schoolhouse in Theik-Pan Road for lunch.

A surprise was waiting. Marjorie told us that Kathleen, Deirdre and Gabriella had come to visit. They sounded like Irish lasses and when I saw them, *longyis* notwithstanding, they were exactly what my friend from Dublin would have called 'fine Mullingar heifers', all three of them with creamy skin and broad hips and that bold way of walking inherent in the girls of Dublin's fair city. They had red hair and green eyes and more freckles between them than any amount of Myint's cream could combat, but in manner and dress they were all Burmese. Auntie May was ready with the explanations.

Kathleen, Deirdre and Gabriella were three of seven daughters whose Irish father had, like William Thomas Townley McHarg, taken up with a Shan girl twenty-odd years ago. They all had Irish names and there was no disguising their Irish blood but they spoke no English at all. Mr O'Rourke, their father, had a small farm five miles from Taunggyi, and the girls came in on market day to do their shopping. They had all been pupils at Auntie May's school and had called in to pay their respects. 'You mean Mr O'Rourke is still around? He hasn't done the dirty on them like my grandfather and gone back to a wife in Galway?' I said to Auntie May. 'Certainly not,' she said. Mr O'Rourke is a respected member of the community. He had entirely foresaken his Irish connections, he didn't want his daughters either to learn English or to become Catholics. What was good enough for the Burmese was good enough for him. I wish we had had time to visit Mr O'Rourke. He sounded an interesting character.

It comes as no surprise that we cannot get places on tomorrow's anti-clockwise flight to Mandalay. I am running short of bribe material – all my cigarettes have been distributed in Theik-Pan Road, and Auntie May has had most of the spare cash which, she assures us, she can change for a colossal rate on the black market – fifty times more than ordinary tourists get in Rangoon. It will have to be the bus. To be honest I would prefer the bus, the memory of that terrifying battering at the hands of Burma Air to Heho was still fresh. Besides, the ten-hour drive would be bound to give us a chance to talk to the locals. Auntie May does not share my enthusiasm for bus travel. 'Wait until you see the bus before you get too excited, Susan,' she advises.

At 5 a.m. next morning, it is still too dark to see anything, even buses, but the vehicle we clamber into could by no stretch of the imagination have been called one. It is an open pick-up truck, not a particularly large pick-up either. Wooden benches have been put at the back, not attached in any way, just short schoolroom benches, the type four-year-old children sit on at Sunday School, and we are packed like sardines, six to a bench. Gaye and I manage to squeeze into one corner of the back seat.

'It is only because Marjorie's husband Peter knows the driver that you were able to get tickets,' whispers Auntie May. 'The bus has been full for two weeks. There is only one bus a day. Two people are having to stand because you have taken their seats.' Stand? This wasn't a number 49 plying its way along Kensington High Street in the rush hour with standing room for five on the lower deck. Where could two extra passengers possibly stand?

We soon find out. A bony, middle-aged man, his *longyi* hoiked up above his knees and a younger man in flapping Chinese trousers were behind the tailgate clutching like limpets on to the back of the truck for the whole of the journey. They must have been incredibly uncomfortable. At the first two-hourly stop for refreshments, Gaye and I offer to change places with the two chivalrous limpets breathing down our necks, but they wave our protests aside with smiles. *Arnadeh* again.

By 10 a.m., it is burningly hot. There is no canopy and the sun beats relentlessly down on our bare heads. Our companions are a silent bunch. I have discovered that the Burmese are incurious, or is it just politeness? They never ask rude questions such as, 'Where are you from?' or 'Where are you going?' or 'Are you on holiday?' Live and let live seems to be the motto and, by the same token, their quiet, reserved expressions do not invite questions. Gaye has the corner seat; the man beside me who is pressed so close against my knees I can feel his sweat running down my leg, keeps his eyes steadily fixed at some spot above the cab. It is only after the third rest-stop, six hours into the journey, that I summon the courage to ask if he lives in Mandalay. What a pity I hadn't found the courage sooner, he is clearly delighted at this unforeseen opportunity to show off his English. It is extremely good.

Yes, he says, he works for the Forestry Department up-country in Maymyo. He came to Heho for two days because his brother's son was having his *shin-pyu*. What a happy coincidence, I tell him. My grandfather, father and stepfather were all in the forestry business in Burma. Had he heard of the book *Elephant Bill*? Certainly, said my companion, it was a classic but it covered a period of colonial rule so you had to hunt hard to find copies. I told him how my grandfather, William Thomas Townley McHarg, had come to Burma eighty years earlier and had become an Assistant District Forest Officer, how my stepfather spoke Burmese and went on tours of duty in the jungle for six weeks at a time with only the *oozies* for company.

If he was impressed, my companion did not show it. It seemed the most natural thing in the world that he should be in the back of a truck next to the granddaughter of someone in the same business as himself. He said elephants were not used for forestry work these days except in the most inaccessible up-country regions. Modern machinery had dispensed with such archaic practices. He also said, sadly, that forestry was a dying industry because the teak trees they were felling were not being replaced at the same rate. There was some experiment with planting fast-growing hardwood trees but the quality was nothing like the traditional wood.

In Rangoon, we had visited a tourist shop and seen some hideous examples of carved teak – huge, clumsy tables with crouching elephants instead of legs, the sort of thing for rich Americans to ship back to their Florida condominiums. Some of the furniture was so huge it didn't look as if it could be moved two feet, let alone 12,000 miles. The shop-owner had enlightened me. It was illegal, he said, to export crude teak. The scam was to carve the wood into such large pieces that after export, the buyer could chop them into whatever shape and size he desired.

I repeated this to my new friend on the truck. He smiled sadly and said everything was changing. Lucrative export contracts were being drawn up with the Japanese. 'We sell them our teak, they sell us arms. It is the new business,' he said and then looked as if he wished he hadn't said so much.

At the next refreshment stop, as we negotiated another primitive outside loo where Gaye warned me to watch out for snakes as I was squatting over the hole (she had seen one disappear down into hers), she remarked casually that the man I had been talking to had a gun. 'A gun? But he works for the Forestry Department,' I said. 'I don't know where he works, but he has definitely got a rifle rolled up in that jacket on his lap,' she said. 'Maybe it is a hunting rifle, but I shouldn't keep questioning him about the political situation if I were you.'

I didn't get the chance. When we clambered back on to our school benches, we had mysteriously been reseated. The Forestry Officer was now one of the two privileged passengers riding in the front cab with the driver. A slight shiver ran down my neck. Was there an official interest being taken in us? Good heavens, maybe the bony old limpet clinging on to the tailgate was a spy! After that, we contented ourselves with gazing out at the exotic landscape bumping along beside us.

Small figures in the fields appeared to be ploughing underwater, the paddy fields were so full of monsoon rain. The ploughs were pulled by pairs of buffalo, the water up to their shoulders, and every time there was a cloudburst, the farmers guiding the ploughs would raise large black umbrellas in the same way as bankers walking down Threadneedle Street might to protect their Savile Row suits.

We stopped for lunch at a rather more elaborate tea-room where we could also get *kauk-sweh*, the traditional Burmese noodles with vegetables. A huge bowlful cost one *kyat*, the green tea was unlimited and free. Gaye was very excited because the owner was clearly a Catholic like herself. There were pictures of baby Jesus being the light of the world, pinned to the matting walls.

It was here that we saw our first example of a black-market tourist, an English girl travelling on her own without money. She survived exclusively on barter. She had the cigarettes and whisky, of course, but also a bundle of cheap nylon T-shirts which she said procured her food and accommodation at a tenth of what we must be paying with regular money. She showed us the T-shirts. They were appalling, the sort of junk you pick up in Brixton Market for 50p each as factory seconds. I suppose I could have forgiven her their inferiority if the designs had not been so unappealing. Huge, garish, multi-coloured Disney figures – Mickey Mouse and Donald Duck plastered all over the fronts. They were an insult to the natural grace and modesty of the Burmese, yet here was Lorraine from Maidstone boasting that a 50p T-shirt could buy her two nights with full board at any hotel from Rangoon to Mandalay. Why, she had even bought a train ticket with a T-shirt, though on the whole she preferred to hitch-hike. She had just arrived on the back of a vegetable lorry. No, that was not worth a T-shirt, the driver had settled for a couple of American cigarettes, but she was now going to sort out a meal with some of her ware. 'Watch me,' she said. We watched.

Lorraine strode to the back of the tea-room where a young man had been regarding us without curiosity. 'Hi there, how you doing? This looks like a neat place. Boy, I can smell home-cooking,' said Lorraine, all friendship and smiles. 'Heh, are there any kids at the back there who might be interested in some really cute T-shirts? The fact is, I am a bit low on funds but these T-shirts would cost you at least £10 in London, so maybe we could come to some arrangement? I could kill a curry and some tea!' The young man inclined his head politely and said there were no young children at the back and he did not want a T-shirt. Lorraine looked offended. 'You can't buy this sort of thing anywhere in Burma, I promise you, this is a unique opportunity. Look, why don't I show you what I have got. In fact, there are only three left, I have been doing such great business with them.' And without waiting to be refused, she dived into her back-pack and pulled out Mickey Mouse, Donald Duck and Pluto. They looked none too clean.

Contrary to what the young man had said, two small boys were peering round the doorway to the back of the tea-room, eyes agog. When they saw Mickey Mouse, they started to laugh. The young man turned and shooed them away like chickens. 'We do not want your T-shirts,' he said to Lorraine. 'We only accept *kyats* for food.'

You had to admire her chutzpah. She didn't give up easily. 'Tell you what, take these round the back and show them to your family and I bet you anything they will want at least one. Take your time, try them on, there is no hurry.' The young man seemed to make up his mind. Without a word he took the three grubby items, holding them slightly away from his body like dead animals, and disappeared into the back. Lorraine joined us at our table. 'It is always the same. They are a bit cautious these Burmese. I don't think they are used to independent girls like me. Had you noticed how all the women scuttle about at the back? God, could you bear to live here? Talk about male chauvinism. Mind you, it is pretty bloody beautiful all the same. Did you see those Flame of the Forest trees back there? Kew Gardens could take a few lessons from this lot.'

While we waited for the negotiations in the rear to yield fruit or at any rate, Lorraine's lunch, she told us about her three weeks in Burma to date. That sounded wrong for a start. Visitors were only allowed to stay one week. Lorraine waved our concerns aside carelessly. 'Listen, they are so primitive out here. They haven't got their act together. How could they possibly check who comes in and who goes out? So I turn up three weeks late at the airport and my entry visa is out of date, so what? I say I have been ill; I say I have had temporary amnesia and can't remember what has happened to me. What are they going to do, lock me up? Ah, here we go; do we have a sale, I wonder?'

The young man was coming towards us holding the T-shirts which had been carefully folded. He put them on the table in front of Lorraine. 'Thank you very much for the offer but no one wishes to take any of your clothing,' he said. 'And by the way, I have to apologise. One of the cooks had a small accident and dropped the one with the Mouse into the cooking pot. I hope it will wash out.'

Lorraine stared open-mouthed, then grabbed the T-shirts and shook them out. Mickey's nether half was covered with thick, brown gravy. 'I am so sorry,' repeated the young man. 'If you can wait, my mother can wash it for you.' Everyone in the tea-room was laughing. Not spitefully, the Burmese are not spiteful, but just naturally as if someone had played a really good joke, which, I suppose, they had. Lorraine flushed. I felt sorry for her. 'Look,' I said, 'you can share our lunch, there is enough here for ten.'

We rattled into Mandalay just before six. At the bus station I climbed unsteadily out of the truck; ten hours on a rough dirt-track with pot-holes the size of heffalump traps every fifty yards takes it out of a body. 'Auntie Sue, Auntie Gaye,' cried a light, childish voice and there was Aye-Aye-Moh, Auntie May's granddaughter, running forward to greet us.

First thing she did was to take our bags, I don't think she even kissed us until she had loaded herself up with our belongings. 'My mummy said you would be thirsty and need a bath so I have arranged to take you to a friend straight away and then we are going to go and have a meal with some other friends who have a television. It arrived last week, I have only seen it once.' She led the way to the horse-drawn rickshaw taxi stand and was piling our bags on the back when I interrupted her. 'Don't worry about the bath, Aye-Aye-Moh, we are booked into the Mandalay Hotel. I am sure we can get everything there and then we will go and see your friends. But come to the hotel with us and we can talk.' So she climbed up beside us and as we trotted through the dusk, she pointed out the sights.

'There is the University, over there. Tomorrow we will go and I will show you where I live. There is the famous Maha Muni Pagoda where tomorrow we will go to wash and wish. There is the Royal Palace with the special water round it. How do you call it? Like a river which is specially built to keep it safe.'

I said she meant a moat and remembered the fantastic story of my great-grandmother, Lady-in-Waiting to Queen Supayalat, swimming across the moat with the giant *lepet* jar. It was a very wide moat.

Aye-Aye-Moh never stopped talking. She was so happy to see us. She longed to come to England. Her friends with the television had a magazine with pictures of London and the things you could buy there. What she really wanted was a pair of pink high-heeled shoes. Everyone said she was a tomboy but this was not true. She wanted pink high-heeled shoes and a dress to go with them.

At the hotel, without being asked, she took it upon herself to unpack our bags and hang up our clothes. Nothing she did appeared subservient or in any way obsequious. It just seemed to come naturally to her as if she was used to helping, to serving, to respecting her elders. If only my children were the same. There was a small crisis when Gaye lost an ear-ring and for half an hour, Aye-Aye-Moh crawled on her hands and knees all over the room searching every inch of tiled floor in bedroom and shower until she found it. 'It is nothing, Auntie Gaye. I like to be of help to you,' she said.

In case you have been wondering why, contrary to Gaye's original proposal, we were not using my Grannie's relatives as an alternative to hotels, the reason was we had not received any invitations to take up. This was *arnadeh* working in reverse if you like. Thinking that their houses couldn't compete with the sort of facilities we were used to at home, my long-lost relatives were sparing us the embarrassment of being polite and having to accept an invitation. That's the way with *arnadeh*. There is so much sensitivity towards other people's feelings in the air in Burma, you need almost a bat-like radar to avoid causing offence. From a purely logistical point of view, the only house in which we might have comfortably stayed was Uncle Pe Kin's in York Avenue. All the others were already full to the brim with permanent house guests. But what they could not offer us in beds, they amply made up for in hospitality and gifts.

The family with the television had given up waiting. When we arrived at their house – less a house than a flat above a shop, their shop – they were all sitting on the floor watching cartoons. The television was still in its box which had been tipped sideways so that the cardboard flaps acted as doors like those walnut-veneered television cabinets for sale at Maples. There was silence in the room. As much concentration as could have been expended on a World Cup Final or the inauguration of a new Pope was now being focused on the antics of Tom and Jerry. The audience, in rows of three deep, were not exclusively children. The head of the family, a portly man, whose black-and-yellow striped *longyi* fell crookedly from his large belly stood, arms folded, at the back of the room with a proprietorial air. When the others laughed uncontrollably as yet again Tom attempts to murder Jerry, U Maung Shweh permitted himself a small, dignified smile.

No one looked up when we slipped into the room. Aye-Aye-Moh, taking the part of a cinema usherette, guided us to a space at the back and until the final familiar 'That's all folks' flashed on to the screen, no one appeared to be aware that visitors had arrived. I have never been a television fan and I know I bore people with my diatribes on the evils of the influence of the small screen on young minds. If the reaction of the family above the shop in Mandalay to our arrival proves anything, it justifies my convictions in part at least. Normally the arrival of visitors in a Burmese home produced a flurry of formality. The children line up waiting to be introduced, the visitor is offered tea, a chair, every sort of consideration. Tom and Jerry changed all that. I am not suggesting we required a trumpet fanfare or a red carpet, it was just interesting to see how a flickering screen (they hadn't had time to fix an aerial) can mesmerise and exclude.

I am not sure how Burmese television worked in those days. There certainly wasn't a continuous programme. This was only the fourth television set to reach Mandalay, hence its fame. Eighty per cent of the programmes were vintage Hollywood films and cartoons, punctuated with news bulletins. 'That's all folks' meant close-down for the rest of that day at any rate, otherwise we would have had to spend the remainder of our evening looking at Lana Turner.

Once the television has been turned off and its cardboard flaps carefully folded down and a large piece of Sellotape fixed to the edges to stop small fingers intruding without permission, the Maung family revert to the characteristic politeness of Burmese hosts. They are all, including U Maung Shweh, enchanted by the tin of Quality Street chocolates I have brought (my mother advised me to pack half a dozen of these as house gifts) and begged to be allowed just one before supper.

Permission was given, this was a special occasion after all. Chocolates are as rare in Burmese households as television. The scene that followed is one I shall never forget. I can still see the expressions on the children's faces as U Maung Shweh slowly and reverently opened the tin lid, taking care not to scratch it. You could hear them holding their breath as he removed the circular top sheet of paper followed by the key and finally there were the jewels themselves in their shiny coloured wrappers. Real gems could not have produced such delight.

Supper follows the same pattern as that first meal we had in Rangoon with Uncle Johnny. The women and children of the household disappear, only U Maung Shweh and a couple of male relatives eat with the three visitors. Without our presence, Aye-Aye-Moh would have been dismissed backstage with the rest of the ladies but now she is permitted to stay strictly as an observer. Her opinions are never sought or offered.

All the children I met in Burma, and not only those of my own relatives, were extraordinarily well-behaved. They never seem to fight. If one were playing with a toy and a sibling came into the room, the first child would offer the toy at once. Squabbling is not part of the Burmese vocabulary. Compare this with the average Western household where sibling rivalry is an established norm and you begin to understand the essential difference between the two forms of upbringing. Even as babies, my children, who, I suspect, are not so very different from any other children in Britain, have grabbed. How many times have I separated screaming toddlers both intent on the same train or tricycle. In Burma, the first words a child learns are 'You can have it' and 'Please take it'. Practically the first words a Western child learns are 'It's mine'. No use pontificating, ours is a competitive society where he who dares wins and to win is all. How long the natural deference of a Burmese child would last in an English playground I shudder to think, but a part of me yearns for the innocence of oriental child-rearing.

We have two days in Mandalay with Aye-Aye-Moh rarely leaving her two aunties. Let me describe her. She is not conventionally pretty but her round face is always alert and ready with a quick smile. She has gleaming, bobbed, jet-black hair, wide-set eyes and a small, rather stocky frame. And she never stops talking. She wants to know all about our family in England. She already knows the genealogy, she has seen photographs but she wants detail, minutiae, trivia. Where do we keep the shoes in our household? Do we have large cupboards in every room? What are the window frames made of? Are the baths really different colours as she has seen in the magazines U Maung Shweh gets sent from his brother who is a doctor in Southend?

Our first port of call after breakfast is the Maha Muni Pagoda containing, it is said, one of only four real-life portraits of the Lord Buddha. Of the others, two are in India, the last in Paradise. The Maha Muni Pagoda isn't as peaceful as Paradise. A ghetto-blaster wired up to a car battery was belting out the Pali version of the Sermon on the Mount, and worshippers scrambled up and down the huge golden Buddha sticking on little squares of gold leaf. You don't pay to light candles in a pagoda, you buy a wafer of gold leaf and add it to the thousands of onion layers already there.

On our way out, we passed stalls selling the usual souvenirs, gongs, bells, holy pictures. Some displayed photographs of the assassinated hero, Aung San, handsome as any modern movie star. Years later when I returned to write a report on the fateful circumstances surrounding his revolutionary daughter Aung San Suu Kyi, these patriotic pictures had been exchanged for new ones of his heroine daughter.

Little things remind me of Aye-Aye-Moh. When I see a pavement half-covered in shade I think of her because she deliberately walked ahead of her two aunties so that we could walk in her shadow and be cool. She never stopped thinking of our wants. Would we like to sit down? Were we tired or thirsty? She would rustle up a chair or a cold drink. Gaye said she wanted to buy a Buddha. There were as many varieties from which to choose as there are Blessed Virgins at Lourdes. We could have had the Lord Buddha in plastic, plaster, wood, ivory or solid gold. We could have had him in any size from charm bracelet to Nelson's Column. The most beautiful, advised Aye-Aye-Moh, were the teak Buddhas finely carved and about eight inches high. She led us to a stall specialising in wood carving and for a pleasant half-hour, we browsed and debated and finally agreed on one each for Gaye and myself.

I couldn't resist a couple of *shin-pyu* head-dresses for the children; they looked like something from conquering Caesar's army, helmet-shaped with cheek and chin pieces, bright silver in colour and tapering at the top to a pagoda spire. Hallowe'ens would never be the same with these on their heads for Trick or Treating.

As the shopkeeper wraps our Buddhas in newspaper and ties them with string, Aye-Aye-Moh appears to be worried. We assure her we will pack them carefully in our suitcases. No, that is not her concern, she has heard us discussing where we will put our carvings. Gaye has said something about the shelf in her hall, I have waxed lyrical about a tableau arrangement I am planning with a collection of elephant ornaments and maybe Lord Buddha somewhere in the middle. 'Please Auntie Sue, when you get home, be sure and place your Buddha high in the room. He must always be the highest thing. It is not good for anything to look down at him so if he is going to stand on a shelf with your elephant ornaments, please raise him above them on a little box. Would you like me to buy you a box?' She was so serious, standing there, so genuine, I took her advice to heart. My elephant tableau has long since been demolished but the Lord Buddha sitting high on a sandalwood box dominates the book-shelf.

My niece's room in Mandalay University is charming. We had wandered through the campus, a collection of shabby, peeling-paint bungalows covered with heavy blossoms, and were now in the residential quarter. Aye-Aye-Moh's dormitory was a long building with arches like a cloister off which were smaller rooms, accommodating four to six girl students. There were no doors and no glass in the windows. For privacy you could pull thin curtains over the openings but in the main people left them open to allow the air to circulate. It can get incredibly hot in Mandalay. My niece's bed had an iron frame reminiscent of my own in the Convent of St Francis de Sales. It looked as though it were part of the same batch; narrow, frugally sprung, with huge casters at the bottom of each leg.

We sat on the end of the bed and Aye-Aye-Moh spread out her belongings for us to inspect. There weren't many. Every student had two shelves which was quite enough for their needs. Aye-Aye-Moh's wardrobe consisted of eight folded *longyis* (seven cotton, one silk for best) and the same number of plain cotton T-shirts. To go with the silk *longyi* she had an embroidered white cotton jacket, the same as the one my mother favours for her Godalming Townswomen's Guild Talk. These were on the bottom shelf. On the top shelf was her Buddha, some flowers and a photograph of the family back in Taunggyí.

As we sat, birds flew in and out of the open windows and perched on the head of the bed. Occasionally her room-mates bustled in and out between lectures. Aye-Aye-Moh had given up her studies for the two days her aunties were visiting. They looked so young, more like primary schoolchildren than university students, and when they chatted to Aye-Aye-Moh their voices were high and light and chirruping like the birds. We dived into our handbags and produced mascaras, lipsticks and any other make-up we could find to give them. Aye-Aye-Moh said Western cosmetics were highly prized in Burma and they thanked us by showing their possessions just as Aye-Aye-Moh had done, more *longyis*, T-shirts and photographs laid out on beds for inspection.

Strolling back through the campus, where little groups of

students were sitting on the grass reading or playing flute-like pipes, I asked Aye-Aye-Moh if she had a boy-friend. 'No Auntie Sue, I am friendly with lots of boys but only because they help me with my business.' Her business? And then it all came out.

Aye-Aye-Moh was a budding entrepreneur. She had a number of business ventures on the go right now, the most lucrative being recycling beer bottles. Another was being a runner for black-market money, I said I didn't want to hear any more, it sounded too dangerous, but Aye-Aye-Moh laughed and said all students had to work to support themselves. They usually did menial jobs like sweeping or cleaning. Beer-bottle recycling and contraband was at least more challenging.

On our last day, my niece took us to the famous monastery at Sagaing – the Burmese equivalent of the seminary at Castel Gandolfo outside Rome. With any luck I might run into cousin Frank, though he would have finished his *phongyi* apprenticeship by now. Sagaing has more than a thousand monks. All monks spend time here in the same way as Roman Catholic priests go to Rome. And then I realised how unrealistic I was being. How would I recognise my cousin whom I had never seen. Uncle Johnny had showed us a photograph of Frank as a child looking solemn and serious in a white school shirt and uniform *longyi* but now he would have his head shaved, the ubiquitous saffron robe and was ten years older. It crossed my mind to stop one of the *phongyis* and ask about my cousin but surely he would not be using his English name here.

What I chiefly remember of our day in Sagaing is climbing steps. Endless wooden steps up the side of a hill to the shrine at the top. This has to be the most inaccessible place of worship, I grumbled to Gaye, who said I must have a short memory. How about all those monasteries we had visited on our ill-fated trip to Ladakh. There was one which was literally perched on the side of a cliff and could only be approached with considerable danger along a narrow, rocky cliff path, much of which had been blown away by storms. Visitors to Sagaing too old or too feeble to make it to the top can stop at minor pagodas dotted at intervals up the hill where you can also get tea. But it was worth the effort. The view from the summit is so peaceful, so tranquil, so untouched by the feverish getting and spending of commerce and the real world. You can see why they chose this site for their seminary.

Back in Mandalay on the way to our next treat we are stuck in a traffic jam, a delightful experience since the traffic consists of bicycles, horse-drawn rickshaws and a few elderly Hillmans. Next stop is the incomparable Kaunghmudaw Pagoda built by a former king as an exact replica of his wife's breast, dazzling white in the sun. White is a sacred colour in Burma. In olden days if you found a white elephant you were exempt from paying taxes for life; only kings could ride white elephants.

We take a boat down the Irrawaddy, the wide wonderful Irrawaddy, and stop at a sandbank for refreshment. A woman brings a watermelon the size of a bicycle wheel and Aye-Aye-Moh launches into a financial deal. If she runs her recycling business as efficiently as she is beating this woman down on the price of the watermelon, she has a great future ahead of her. There is much arm waving and eyebrow raising and short, incredulous gasps, but eventually the deal is struck. We pick up the watermelon, we exclaim, we smile and everyone seems happy when Aye-Aye-Moh hands over eight *kyats*, especially the vendor. Aye-Aye-Moh, who carries as much in her small Shan bag as a boy scout packs in his rucksack for a week, produces a knife and expertly cuts the watermelon into manageable segments. We sit on the sand with our feet trailing in the water munching the sweet, juicy heart of the melon and I feel this must be as near to Paradise as I shall ever get. 'If you see a snake, Auntie, be sure and pull your feet in,' says Aye-Aye-Moh. 'Remember, a bite from a watersnake is always fatal.' Paradise lost at a stroke. Even if the snakes were harmless I would run. I have inherited my mother's phobia fostered by the plumbing at the Mission School at Moulmein.

8

Pagan

Next morning at the airport, we are peremptorily advised by the Burma Air clerk that there are no seats on the Mandalay –Pagan flight. It is no use showing him our confirmed flight tickets. We had stopped at the Burma Air counter the day before to make absolutely sure we were on the list. A group of Japanese businessmen – he said the word businessmen with emphasis, implying that they were of rather more use to the nation than a pair of independent lady travellers – were taking up most of the seats. This was potentially catastrophic. Pagan was as far away as Taunggyi and we had no bus reservations either. If we missed this flight we would have to abandon our trip to Pagan. My purpose for visiting Burma was to see my long-lost relatives but for a visitor such as Gaye, a trip to Burma without visiting Pagan was as unthinkable as visiting Agra and missing out the Taj Mahal.

Aye-Aye-Moh sizes up the situation in a flash. She takes me aside and whispers urgently, 'Auntie Sue, are you sure you have no more Marlboro cigarettes in your bag? Two packets would be enough.' I am not a smoker but Gaye is

175 •

and there was nothing for it but to dip into her personal supply. From now on, she could smoke indigenous cheroots. Aye-Aye-Moh takes two of Gaye's three remaining packets of Benson & Hedges and with a demure air approaches the Burma Air clerk. Their heads are bent low. They look as though they are praying together, not handing over bribes, but minutes later the clerk disengages himself from my niece and returns to his desk. *Longyis* don't have pockets, he isn't carrying the cigarettes but neither is Aye-Aye-Moh, so he must have slipped them down the front of his shirt. No matter, what we are really interested in are the two boarding passes he now hands over with a ghost of a smile.

There is great excitement at the Departure Lounge: the famous Burmese actress, May Sweet, is there with her boy-friend. The importance of the visiting aunties is immediately put into perspective; we are not half as important as this glimpse of a glamorous actress and Aye-Aye-Moh excuses herself to join the autograph queue.

Our flight is called. Aye-Aye-Moh, thank heavens, does not subject us to the sort of Hollywood farewell scene we have experienced with Auntie Betty and Auntie May. She is matter-of-fact. 'Write to me every week, Auntie Sue, and come back to Burma soon and if it is possible you could send us a television, we would love you very much. It would be good to have a television.' Well, at least she isn't bumping round my knees in a rattling go-kart but this obsession to own television sets is disturbing. She gives us both quick hugs and we make our way to the plane and, happily, a problem-free flight. No elastic bands on this machine.

The Japanese businessmen and a large group of American tourists have beaten us to the Thiripyitsaya, the only hotel for Westerners in Pagan. The alternative we are told is accommodation in the village. Someone directs us to the Mo-Mo Guest House on the main street next to a grocery shop and a higgledy-piggledy assortment of corrugated iron sheeting which turns out to be someone's house.

My children would have loved the Mo-Mo Guest House; it was like the houses they used to build in the garden with blankets and sheets, a cross between a wigwam and a bedouin tent. Instead of blankets and sheets, the preferred building material here was plaited coconut matting. Our bedroom walls were made of the same, there was a bamboo door and when the man in the next room undressed for the night, you could hear every detail of his clothing being removed, every button undone, shoelace untied. But we are delighted with our two low beds with lumpy mattresses and a single cotton sheet. It is late but the sounds outside of people promenading are irresistible so we forget our plans for an early night to enable us to rise at dawn and see the magnificent pagoda skyline. Out we go.

There are more than a thousand pagodas in Pagan built over a huge area with the village occupying a tiny corner and the Thiripyitsaya Hotel a couple of miles away on its own. Presumably the tourists are tucked up in bed or drinking gin in the hotel cocktail bar for the people strolling along the village street are all local. So much is happening. There are dozens of stalls lit with hurricane lamps offering souvenirs suitable for Westerners and Burmese alike, for Pagan is a place of pilgrimage for all Buddhists. We have our Buddhas and our *shin-pyu* hats and more Shan bags than we know what to do with and are content to window-shop until we come across a stall selling puppets. There must be forty different models, all of them representing characters in an ancient drama similar to the fall of Troy.

What I should really like is the original play to understand who these exotic figures represent and why they are carrying such weird accessories but that will have to come later. The girl in the stall unhooks the Princess, the General, the Magician, the Witch and shows us their finer points. The finer point of the jester, she gigglingly demonstrates as she lifts the folds of his *longyi*, is a huge wooden phallus. This is for sale only to the gentlemen, she says, showing us the one she offers lady tourists which has a member the size of a pencil stub. They are all hand-made, their limbs little more than wooden blocks approximating to torso, leg and arm joints. It is their clothing that amazes. The General, for instance, is all pink satin and sequins, his sword is silver, his shoes padded silk with pointed toes like goblins'. On his head he wears a miniature helmet encrusted with gems and the expression on his painted face is pure evil.

'How much is the General?' I ask. Fifty *kyats*, replies the girl, around five pounds or fifty pounds on the Rangoon black market, nearer two hundred with Auntie May's contacts. She looks expectantly at us waiting for the usual haggling session to begin but I am not inclined to haggle. The General is a work of art. In Bangkok airport, the gift shops were selling Thai puppets based on the ancient Siamese legends. They were ten times the price of this and factory-made.

I open my purse and the girl sees a five-pound note which excites her as much as the General has excited me. 'This is good,' she says. 'You give me this.' She must have black-market contacts too. She also sees the plastic comb that came with my British Airways travel-bag. Can she have it, her hand gestures imply?

So for five pounds and a plastic comb, I now have a family treasure that never fails to arouse interest in every visitor to our house. The mechanics alone are awe-inspiring. Every joint, including finger-joints, has its own string, a skilled puppeteer could choreograph a sophisticated ballet for it, so lifelike and flexible are its movements. All the strings are attached to a piece of crude wood which looks like part of a twig snapped off from the nearest tree. The girl wraps the General, not in tissue as they would have done in Bangkok or newspaper in Mandalay – such niceties don't exist in Pagan. Instead she wraps it in what she takes presumably to be rags but to me are beautiful pieces of woven material which I shall turn into a wall-hanging when I get home. Delighted with my purchase and not at all sorry to lose the plastic comb, we sit in a tea house and drink green tea until midnight.

The following day is devoted to pagoda-crawling. The conventional way to do this is in a horse-drawn rickshaw with, if you are prepared to pay for it, an English-speaking guide who will explain the finer points of every pagoda. The Dhammayangyi Temple for instance, black and sinister, has an equally terrifying history. The story goes that King Narathu the Terrible, who had commissioned it, went on a tour of inspection when it was not yet complete. His sharp eyes saw something. He ordered a minion to fetch a needle and forced it between two bricks. 'There should be no gaps in the walls of my pagoda,' he raged and had the architect summarily beheaded.

Some of the pagodas are little more than beach huts in size, others so crumbling that if the rickshaw were to reverse into them, they would probably collapse. However, the larger ones, heavily annotated in the tourist guides, are magnificent and we could have spent a day in each. Because we only have one day for everything, we soldier on through the intense heat of the afternoon when all sensible people are taking siestas. By sunset, the recognised hour to sit and watch the wonderful changing colours of the sky behind the variegated heights and shapes of the thousand spires, we are all but done in.

I cannot pretend to do justice to the glory of Pagan in two pages. The sadness is that if this inspires you to visit – be warned. Pagan has changed almost beyond recognition. The pagodas are still there, but the surrounding landscape has suffered dramatic, most would say calamitous, change.

Five years after my first visit I returned to Pagan and looked for the Mo-Mo Guest House. It didn't seem to be there, nor the bus-stop beside it where on my last visit people had queued at 2 a.m. for the overnight bus to Meiktila. There was no Guest House, no bus-stop, no street, no village; they had all been flattened by bulldozers the month before and the inhabitants relocated to an arid plain four miles away. This was phase one of the Government's draconian measures to attract more tourists to Burma. The site where the picturesque but ramshackle village once stood was now destined to accommodate half a dozen luxury hotels. For the planned influx of tourists, 1996 has been designated Visit Myanmar Year. When I went to Burma the first time, the annual quota of visitors was around 6000. This year they are hoping for half a million.

The charm of Pagan was the feeling that it had not been touched by what we recognise as progress. There were no tarmac roads, no snack bars, other than the indigenous tea stalls, no facilities in the accepted sense of modern tourism. When you climbed into your rickshaw, it was up to the driver to decide which way he would go and where, in what order. Now, I understand, just as the two Burma Air planes go clockwise or anti-clockwise, there are to be conventional itineraries: the short tour, the longer scenic route, the Narathu the Terrible and Other Examples of Barbaric Kings tour. I am glad I saw it the way it was.

We have a plane to Rangoon the following afternoon which allows us, if we are quick and make an early start, sufficient time to visit Mount Popa first. I am doing this for my mother. Mount Popa is another sacred place of pilgrimage for Buddhists. It has the added attraction of an extraordinary natural phenomenon in the form of pagoda stones. I have mentioned my mother's penchant for jewels. But the only items of jewellery I remember from those early days in Kenton were our pagoda-stone rings. They were simple, a slim band of gold with one small milky stone in which, if you looked hard, you could make out the silhouette of a pagoda.

All the stones on Mount Popa, my mother assured me, had this pagoda image naturally inside them. A geologist would probably be able to explain why the image appears when the stone is polished. Maybe in a Moslem country the pagoda image would be described as a minarette or in New Mexico as a totem pole. There is no official transport to Mount Popa, an hour's drive from Pagan, so we hitch a ride in a truck and get there in time for breakfast. It is Sagaing in miniature, endless steps up a very steep hill but without the minor pagodas or the seminary. Disconcertingly, a back-packer from Auckland has beaten us to it and attaches himself to us uninvited. He is wearing a straw hat with corks and tells us that every cork represents a country he has back-packed in. Enough said.

I pick up handfuls of what looks like gravel searching for a suggestion of a pagoda in every pebble. It all looks like gravel to me. Maybe when they are polished they will yield the same milky stones that my mother keeps in her jewel box but I am doubtful. We climb to the top of the steps and an airy gazebo construction where monkeys are swinging casually on the wooden rafters. One of them uses my shoulder as a spring-board and the smell of the animal is horrible. I had no idea monkeys were so heavy, they look like little balls of koala fluff but they pack a punch when they land four-square on your shoulder.

As we regain our breath and bearings, a monk, who has been watching our ascent, approaches. He asks if we have a cigarette for him. Gaye obliges and, rummaging in my bag for a light, I drop a coin. The monk bends and picks it up, examines it on both sides and says at last, 'Whose head is this?' I tell him it is Queen Elizabeth II of England. 'Are you English?' he wants to know. I tell him proudly that I have two Burmese grandmothers but this does not appear to interest him in the least. 'And is your friend English?' he says, inclining his head at Gaye. Gaye explains that she is Irish and produces some Irish coins from her purse explaining that her money is different from mine. Once again the monk examines the proffered coin – it is an Irish threepenny piece.

'And is the King of Ireland a rabbit?' he says, pointing to the image on the penny. (Irish coins go in for native fauna.) He laughs uproariously. We laugh too. It is a good joke. The man with the cork hat who has caught us up (he stopped half-way to buy what he thought looked like the Burmese equivalent of a cork) wants to know what all the laughing is about and the monk is delighted to give him a rerun.

I show our new friend the stones I am taking home to polish in pursuit of pagoda jewellery. The monk shakes his head. 'This is just dirt,' he says. 'What are these rings you are talking about?' I explain the saga of the pagoda stones and he looks unconvinced. He has never heard of pagoda stones. On the other hand he has only been at the Mount Popa Monastery for a month, his home is south of Rangoon and he will be returning to his own monastery after three months, so maybe he is unaware of the local phenomenon.

For the first time, we see female *phongyis*. With their shaved heads and asexual saffron robes they are almost indistinguishable from the men, except that they are wearing bright-red lipstick and some have painted their toe-nails to match. This reminds me that we are due to meet my niece, Susan, who is even now paying off her debt for her physics degree in some nunnery. She will, no doubt, tell us the finer details of monastic life when we meet her in Molet Saung Gong tomorrow.

There is a hitch. When we return to Pagan airport we are informed that once again the flight is full. This time, no amount of cigarettes, even if we had them to spare, would change the situation. Two American tour groups have arrived and even some of these are having to spend an extra night in Pagan. We ask if there is room on the clockwise plane which would mean getting to Rangoon via Mandalay and Heho, but this too is overbooked. There is no question of us spending an extra night in Pagan, our seven-day visas run out in thirty-six hours and we haven't the confidence of Lorraine from Maidstone to talk our way out of a tight corner.

The only alternative is the train. If we are quick we can catch a bus to the terminal at Thazi, three hours' drive from Pagan, and pick up the Over-Night Express from Mandalay to Rangoon. This time it really is a bus. It stops at villages where girls with trays of fruit walk up and down outside the windows offering refreshment. Some of the fruits we have never seen before, small yellow berries the size of cherries but very bitter. Huge green plums with a peculiar tang that distinguishes them from greengages.

It is 10 at night when we get to Thazi and all hell seems to be breaking loose at the station. It doesn't look as if there has been a train for a week. There are people on the platform who appear to be living there, they have cooking pots and washing hanging on make-shift washing lines. We ask someone where the ticket office is. He points to a queue which snakes its way twice round the station and on down towards the town. Our hearts sink but we are advised that without a ticket we will be thrown off the train. There is a subdued air about the people queuing and we are not inclined to talk much. Half the passengers are soldiers toting huge back-packs and rifles, the others are a mixture of traders, businessmen and old couples.

The train is two hours late, presumably because it took that extra time to stack all the passengers on board. I have never seen so many people on a train. They are everywhere, five to a seat intended for two, on each other's laps, in the central aisle, sitting or lying in the luggage racks. When we bought our tickets, we had asked if we could reserve a seat. No wonder the booking clerk gave us an amused look. This is one of those old-fashioned trains like the ones you see in John Wayne movies rattling across the mid-West where you have to jump from one coach to the next. There was no question of staying where we were. Compared to this mêlée, rush hour on the Northern Line is a doddle.

Slowly and cumbersomely we inched our way through the press of bodies. Sometimes the blockage was so impenetrable we had to wait patiently while passengers unpacked themselves to afford a passage-way through. There was one first-class carriage whose incumbents lolled back in their seats allowing only one or two lucky passengers to squat at their feet. For one exciting moment we thought we had actually spotted an empty space. A young soldier with a single red star over his left-hand pocket had vacated a window space after a quick exchange with his neighbour. He must have had a second-class ticket or something. He had hardly got out of it when a woman carrying two small children pushed past and claimed it. Two *phongyis* in the seats opposite in dark-red robes (dark-red instead of saffron seems to be the uniform of senior monks) continued with their reading, taking no interest in any of this. In the luggage rack above them, next to the baggage, were their two wooden begging bowls. One was deep in a cartoon comic, the other flicked through a magazine in which I could just make out pictures of Maradona.

With incredible dexterity, traders carrying trays of food were managing to pass up and down the jam-packed aisles, hoping for sales. I wanted to buy a couple of interesting-looking cakes which smelt of sesame – we hadn't eaten since breakfast thanks to all the messing around at the ticket office. But Gaye cautioned, wisely as it turned out, that we should find somewhere to sit before the next station, so on we went until we got to the end of the carriage and the appalling prospect of leaping over the gap in pitch darkness to the next coach.

My eyesight at the best of times is pretty useless. At night I have a little more than mole vision but needs must when the devil drives, so I took a deep breath and launched myself across the coupling to the swaying silhouette ahead. It was oddly exhilarating, maybe not quite as exhilarating for the heap of sleeping bodies on whom I landed, but they didn't complain. This seemed to be a section of the train where the fast-food vendors collected. We bought a selection of samosa-style snacks and stood by the rail looking out into the gloom while we ate them. This carriage was, if possible, even more intensely packed than the last. No chance of anywhere to sit, stand or squat so on we went to our next flying leap and our third coach. The train was not scheduled to stop for another couple of hours. All that talk about being thrown off if we hadn't got a ticket was hot air. It would have taken a ticket collector a week to check this lot.

At what stage we decided to give up the unequal struggle of looking for somewhere commodious to pass the rest of the night I cannot say. It may just have been that we ran out of train. The only place we could find six inches of floor space was outside the lavatory in the carriage behind the engine. I will not describe the various murky substances leaking beneath the door, better not to think of those if we were to snatch any sleep. So we sat on our cases and leaned against each other and became accustomed to people climbing over us for urgent purposes. From where I sat, I could see the occupants of the seats adjacent to me. There were four men snoring fitfully, their *longyis* loosened round their waists, their legs stretched out, while under the seats you could just make out the figures of four sleeping women lying on the floor. From now on, I thought, I shall never complain if a man does not offer me his seat on the tube. Permission to lie under the seat is what we Burmese feminists are fighting for.

The most impressive thing about the journey was how rarely people complained. You can imagine how Disgruntled Tunbridge Wells would have reacted to this shambles. Snorts and sniffing and threats to write a letter to *The Times*. These Burmese passengers accepted their conditions without grumbling. As for the children, and there were babes in arms aplenty, they slept on, sucking their fingers.

At first light, a significant change came over the compartment. Everyone was engaged in the business of rising and shining and the carriage took on a purposeful air. We must have got rid of a few passengers along the line because the place looked distinctly less chock-a-block. The four ladies who had been lying under the seats uncurled themselves and emerged blinking and stretching. They then began a dauntingly elaborate and efficient toilette, achieved in remarkably little time and space. They brushed their teeth with tiny wooden toothbrushes, using water from bottles the size of nail varnish pots. They spat daintily into even smaller bowls which they seemed to have about their persons. Then one of their group volunteered to take all the bowls and throw the contents out of the window. As they worked, they chatted and giggled like teenagers preparing for a party.

Next came the make-up, *thanaka* of course, produced from small plastic compacts and applied with tiny wadges of cotton wool reminiscent of my mother's famous matchbox toy. They put perfume behind their ears and at their wrists and then commenced the complicated restyling of their hair. Burmese ladies have wonderful hair: thick, black, straight and so glossy with coconut oil, it looks permanently wet. The four ladies unpinned the coils that had come unravelled by sleep and, holding the pins between their teeth, combed their tresses back into shape with wooden combs whose teeth were set as wide apart as garden rakes. All this they did unselfconsciously and without the self-satisfied preening one sees in women putting on their make-up in Ladies' Powder Rooms in the West.

Finally they attended to their clothes. I don't know how they did it but with the minimum of dabbing and brushing and flicking they managed to make the *longyis* and blouses they had been sleeping in on the floor all night look as though they had just come back from the cleaners. Being tiny must have something to do with it. There wasn't room for the dirt to linger. Meanwhile even more exciting things were happening by the window.

Two young men, whose luggage consisted of nothing but coarse hessian sacks knotted at one end, were behaving most suspiciously. They seemed to be operating a highly organised form of delivery service in which precise timing was of paramount importance. One had his head stuck out of the window and then without turning round would wave at his companion who picked up a sack and heaved it through the opening. To judge by the way the contents bulged, it looked as though the sacks contained some sort of fine sand. My curiosity overcame me and I went to the adjoining window to see what was going on. It was a primitive courier service.

Every so often, a figure would appear by the side of the track and wave, which was the signal for another sack to be heaved out. The courier would then pick up the sack and scuttle out of sight. We must have done twenty drops before we reached the outskirts of Rangoon, by which time I had composed an entire scenario of a multi-million-*kyat* drugs racket, marginally more complex than the French Connection.

No one else in the compartment was taking any notice of these shenanigans. They had doubtless seen it hundreds of times before. When the train finally pulled into Rangoon station, the two young smugglers got out and strolled off as nonchalantly as day-trippers. As for the four young women, they had produced high-heeled sandals from their Shan bags and were now click-clacking smartly off like Essex-girl secretaries on their way to the office. Not even Sherlock Holmes could have guessed that they had spent the night on the floor of a bumping train. Every trace of the journey had been erased, they looked as fresh and fragrant as morning jasmine still covered with dew. I wish I could have said the same about myself. I didn't want to look too closely at my shoes and the bottom of my case was exuding a powerful odour compared to which *balachan*, that pungent Burmese pickle made from dried shrimps, garlic and oil, smelt like Chanel No.5.

Our time in Burma was drawing to a close. We had two definite engagements: dinner with the British Ambassador that evening and another jaunt out to Molet Saung Gong on our way to the airport to meet Susan, my niece. There was a minor crisis at the Strand when, unpacking our suitcases to find our party frocks for dinner at the British Embassy, Gaye discovered that her jar of Auntie May's *balachan* had leaked. No amount of scrubbing or squirts with the scent bottle could get rid of that all-pervasive smell of drains. In the end, I lent her my second-best dress, poured her the last of our duty-free gin and by the time the Embassy car came to collect us, we had recovered our spirits.

We step into a grey vintage Daimler and are swept away to a magnificent old colonial house built originally for the manager of the Irrawaddy Flotilla Company. A Burmese cat stalks through the door ahead of us and a Bach oratorio is flooding the ante-ante-room. Mrs Fenn, the Ambassador's wife, cool, blonde and beautiful in sugar-pink organza, rises from a deep sofa to greet us. Our man in a short-sleeved shirt, Nicholas Fenn, tells us that Rangoon was his first diplomatic posting twenty years earlier and ever since then he and Susan had been trying to winkle their way back. They both speak fluent Burmese.

Burma, says Mr Fenn without a trace of pomposity or patronage, is a blushing flower surrounded by weeds – he tactfully declines to mention India, Bangladesh, Laos, China and Thailand – which threaten to choke it. It needs protecting but it is quite simply the most beautiful, unspoilt country on earth. My sentiments entirely on that first visit. Next day, we left Rangoon laden with enough Shan bags, woven purses, embroidered hats, jars of *balachan* and packets of prawn crackers (my mother's favourite) to open an ethnic boutique.

On the way to the airport we stopped off at Molet Saung Gong to say hail and farewell to my twenty-one-year-old niece Susan who was being allowed time off from her six months as a *phongyi*. It was a curious encounter. She looked just like the other nuns we had seen at Mount Popa, with the same shaved head and even the same bright lipstick. Her English was as fluent as Auntie Betty's, but she lacked Aye-Aye-Moh's entrepreneurial self-confidence, and giggled shyly behind her hand. Praying, she admitted, had got her good results, but she was reticent about what the future might hold when she returned to the world. What she would really like, she confessed between more embarrassed giggles, would be to come and visit me in England. Was it something I could arrange. I promised I would do my best. You can guess who turned up at the airport for the final goodbye. The Botataung clan were there in force, but so this time was Auntie Betty who had managed to get an official permit.

My final memory as we walked towards the aeroplane is of Betty with her sad, beautiful face blinking away tears, waving a white handkerchief, saying, 'Come back soon, Susan. Next time bring your mummy with you.'

9

Myanmar

That all happened ten years ago. Since then, I have been back to Burma twice, once with my husband and the last time in July 1990 to write a piece for the *Observer* about the current political situation.

Much has happened in those five years. Aung San Suu Kyi, daughter of Burma's first independent leader Aung San, assassinated along with eight members of his Cabinet in 1947, has become Burma's new national heroine. In 1988, she had returned to Rangoon (she is married to an Oxford don) to look after her sick mother and been caught up in the student revolution. She was elected General Secretary of the opposition party, the National League for Democracy, and was placed under house arrest by SLORC, the State Law and Order Restoration Council, the name used by the new military dictatorship under General Saw Maung. (General Ne Win had retired as Burma's supremo the previous year but was still the *éminence grise* behind the premiership). Despite Aung San Suu Kyi's detention, the National League for Democracy had just won a landslide victory in May 1990, but instead of her taking her rightful place as head of government, her detention order was extended and the NLD outlawed.

Terrible stories came out of Burma about the atrocities committed by the army in the name of keeping the peace. The student demonstrations in Rangoon met with the same indiscriminate killings as those in Tiananmen Square the following summer. Amnesty International published horrifying statistics about the number of people detained, tortured and executed by the new regime; all the universities were officially closed in 1988 and those NLD members who had not been arrested fled the country.

Curious as it may seem, the effect all this political upheaval had on my Burmese relatives was negligible. The annual Christmas cards, spangly affairs showing pagodas against the sunset, the envelopes covered with exotic stamps, continued to reach us. The letters inside contained the usual domestic news, a new baby, another death. My mother and stepfather had visited Burma the year after me and though I suspect from my mother's point of view the visit was not entirely comfortable – she made withering comments about the primitive state of her cousin and her half-sister's houses – at least they seemed to write to each other more frequently thereafter.

What did change was our ability to communicate with them. Letters addressed to Burma instead of Myanmar were returned marked 'Country Unknown'. Our annual Red Cross parcels at Christmas time arrived minus most of their contents. The ten pounds my mother used to send Auntie May every month in a letter went missing so many times, a new highly complex system worthy of Le Carré had to be devised. As far as I can make out it involved the Diplomatic Bag, a dead-letter drop and a friend of a friend of a Shan princess in Rangoon, whom Auntie May once taught to sing 'Silent Night'. But at least they all appeared to be safe. The closure of the universities had temporarily put an end to Aye-Aye-Moh's studies; she was back in Taunggyi working as a greeter in a restaurant specialising in wedding breakfasts.

Going back for the paper in 1990 put me back in touch. More than ever was it necessary to disguise my profession – journalists were definitely unwelcome in Burma the year of the ill-fated elections. It was illegal to talk to foreign journalists. Since the Burmese Embassy in London knew who I was by now, I went through elaborate hoops to get a visa. Using my married name on my new passport with 'housewife' in the profession box, I applied for a visa at the Embassy in Vienna, and armed with the usual chocolates, cosmetics and cigarettes, went back in, every inch the investigative reporter. My mother was fearful. On no account must I compromise Auntie May or any of the other members of the family. Auntie Betty had died two years earlier, so at least she was safe.

This time I did not have the luxury of Uncle Pe Kin seeing me through Customs. Along with everyone else I had my luggage searched twenty-five times and when I unpacked in my room at the Strand, I discovered that all the cosmetics I had brought for presents had been snaffled. It must have been the stony-faced woman at the last search. She had spent more than usually long digging into my possessions and mysteriously had made me fill in an extra form. Presumably while I was doing that, she had bagged my lipsticks. Oh well, Aye-Aye-Moh, Marjorie and Susan would have to do without this time. But I felt rattled just the same.

The Strand Hotel, if anything, had deteriorated since my last visit. At dinner when I was handed a menu with twenty-five main dishes of which twenty-three had been crossed out, the choice was between omelettes and chicken curry. The lift didn't seem to work either; one thing had improved, however, you got a lot more *kyats* for your sterling on the black market. On my last trip I was offered six times the official rate; this time the porter who carried my case upstairs whispered that he knew somebody who could offer me fifteen times as much.

There was a message waiting for me. It was from Tourist Burma who seemed to have a much stronger hold on visitors' itineraries than in the old, relaxed days. There were no flights to Heho and they had booked me on the seven o'clock train to Pagan next morning and arranged a room for me at the Thiripyitsaya Hotel. This was not what I had planned. I had gifts for Auntie May but what I really wanted to do was quiz Aye-Aye-Moh about the student demonstrations in Taunggyi.

I telephoned the Tourist Burma office at once. A polite voice answered. It was impossible for me to fly to Heho; there was only one plane a week and it was completely booked with a waiting list. 'But I thought there were two planes a day, clockwise and anti-clockwise . . .' I protested. The polite voice said that there had never been more than one plane a week. We were rewriting history already. 'But I don't want to go to Pagan, I have been to Pagan before and I particularly want to see Taunggyi,' I said. The polite voice explained patiently that all the arrangements had been made, I would be collected from the Strand Hotel at 6.15 in the morning and escorted to the station. It sounded like a threat. Oh well, there must be one or two pagodas I had missed.

Next I telephoned Uncle Johnny in Botataung. 'How about me coming over to see you, I haven't got a television but I have got some cigarettes,' I said. Uncle Johnny, also sounding polite, said it would be nice but impossible because of the curfew. No one was allowed in the streets after dark. It was now dark.

Things really had changed. I resigned myself to the omelette, joined two Russian businessmen in the bar afterwards for a vodka, and had an early night. The Russians were there putting in a tender for a new packaging factory. They said the stiffest competition was coming from the Koreans, followed by the Chinese. Yes, there was a lot of foreign investment in Burma under the new government. Most of the teak concessions had been sold to the Japanese. 'You mean natural teak in planks?' I said, remembering the man in the gift shop who had told me about exporting large pieces of furniture to chop up elsewhere. Yes, planks, lots of planks, laughed the Russians.

The Tourist Burma guide waiting in the lobby at 6.15 the next morning did not look as though he had laughed for a long time. He handed me two cardboard boxes; one, he said, contained my breakfast, the other my lunch. It was a ten-hour train journey to Thazi, the rail connection to Pagan. 'I know, I know, you don't have to tell me,' I said and started to describe the nightmare journey I had made on that same train five years before. He listened without comment. He was really very spooky.

By the time we reached the station, both my cardboard boxes had collapsed. No wonder they were inviting tenders for a new packaging factory. The guide found my reserved first-class seat. How different it was from the last time I had travelled on the Rangoon–Thazi express. There was hardly anyone on the train. Was it going to be possible for me to get from Pagan to Taunggyi, I asked, as he prepared to leave. He gestured enigmatically and said a message would be left at the hotel in Pagan. 'Have a nice day,' he added, like a waitress at an American drive-in. I supposed they all had televisions now and had picked up the jargon.

I looked out of the window; on the platform was one of the Government's huge, red propaganda signs. This one said: 'Co-operate To Preserve Military Peace and Tranquillity.' I had noticed many like it coming in from the airport the night before. 'Thanks for my lunch,' I said.

At Toungoo, half-way to Thazi, a very senior army officer, to judge by all the ribbons on his chest, got on and sat in the seat diagonally across the aisle from me. As we departed there was much heel-clicking and saluting from the soldiers on the platform. In the small open area behind our carriage, outside the lavatory, a skinny private stood guard over a bag of golf clubs along with the officer's kit. Lolling back in his seat set at the 'recline' position, a paperback copy of *On Golden Pond* on his lap, dark glasses, cigarette drooping from languid fingers, the officer looked every inch the Riviera sophisticate, sunning himself on an Antibes beach. Except for his bootlaces. The boots themselves were impeccable: black, patent and shiny, but the laces were too short and only reached half-way. 'Never Hesitating, Always Ready to Sweat Blood and Tears is the Tatmadaw' declared a government slogan beside the track. Tatmadaw means Army. Its representative across the aisle didn't look as if he had even perspired.

I have already told you how they bulldozed the village at Pagan and the Mo-Mo Guest House, not that I would have been allowed to stay there anyway. My orders were to report to the Thiripyitsaya Hotel and, in case I had any plans to defect, another Tourist Burma guide was waiting for me when I got off the bus. They could have saved themselves the bother of reserving me a room. I was the only guest in the hotel. Whatever else the political turmoil had done, it had certainly knocked the stuffing out of the tourist trade. Imagine finding yourself alone in the Piazza San Marco or on top of the Acropolis in August.

I might have guessed Auntie May, the omniscient Auntie May, wouldn't let me down. I had been in my room barely five minutes before the telephone rang. It was Auntie May. Realising I would not be able to fly to Heho, she had made a contingency plan. Aye-Aye-Moh was on her way by pick-up to meet me. It was a pity, she said at the end of the crackling line, because she had prepared my favourite meal – *kauk-sweh*, *mo-hin-ga* and *buthe-gyaw* – and she had invited Myint and her husband to join us, but there it was. There was no point in arguing with fate, you just had to rearrange your plans. So the mountain's representative was coming to Mohammed on the bus.

It was three years since I had last seen Aye-Aye-Moh. It was not so much her appearance that had changed as her demeanour. There was a wariness about her which hadn't been there before. She still chattered away non-stop, she still exuded the same energy, but that delightful habit of breaking into a wide, infectious smile had gone. She was twenty-two, she had not completed her degree at Mandalay University because, in her final year, all the universities had been closed following student demonstrations. I said I had heard that there were demonstrations at Taunggyi too. Could she tell me about them? Immediately the shutters came down. 'It was nothing really, Auntie Sue, just a few people in the streets, but it was nothing. Tell me, how is Auntie Jenny, how are all her children?' It was obvious she did not want to talk about political affairs. For the moment I let it rest. The most important thing right now was to see if I could arrange transport to Taunggyi. The Tourist Burma guide had said he would be back in the morning to take us for a conducted pagoda tour. We would have to work on him then.

There was a difficult moment when I went to the reception desk to book a room for Aye-Aye-Moh for the night. Without the flicker of an eyelid, the clerk replied that this would not be possible, the hotel was full.

'But I am the only person staying,' I said.

'I am sorry, it is full, we are expecting a large tour later this evening. It is full,' he insisted.

'Well, that is no problem, she can stay in my room. I have twin beds,' I said triumphantly.

Momentarily flummoxed he may have been but not flattened. 'The Thiripyitsaya Hotel is for foreign tourists, not for Burmese nationals,' he said.

'So where do Burmese nationals have to stay when they visit Pagan?' I wanted to know.

'At one of the guest houses in the village,' he replied automatically and then stopped short. We both realised he had fallen into his own trap. The bulldozing of the village was so recent an event he had forgotten to take it into consideration. Without another word, he handed Aye-Aye-Moh a registration card. It was a minor skirmish but I had won and I felt elated.

Dinner in the echoing dining-room was a lonely business. The reception clerk may have been expecting a large tour group but the dining-room staff certainly were not. None of the other tables was laid. We had an indifferent meal (oh for the *kauk-sweh*, *mo-hin-ga* and *buthe-gyaw* Auntie May had prepared), and talked in whispers. Aye-Aye-Moh was still working at the restaurant where she had been promoted to manageress. She had expanded the wedding business, she told me, and made it more up-to-date. The banqueting suite had been redecorated, she had found new musicians. The ones they had before played only traditional Burmese music, but their replacements, she said proudly, were more like a pop group.

I ask for news of her family. She says Toto, now eighteen, is an apprentice for a West German engineering company in Syriam, the other side of the river from Rangoon. Maybe we could visit him. Her mother, my cousin Marjorie, has been in hospital. She had breast cancer, a common complaint among Burmese women, and has had one of hers removed. Auntie May was just the same, perhaps a little more bad-tempered, but as usual on the look-out for a financial deal. Yes, she was still playing Mah-jong every evening in the Chinese Quarter – it was an important part of the family income, said Aye-Aye-Moh, she was so good at it.

'Please Auntie Sue, will you see about a ticket for me to come to England some time? It cannot be until next year, I have to look after my mother while she is ill but I should like to come.' This was a new departure. Aye-Aye-Moh had never expressed any interest in leaving Burma. She may have wanted the material advantages of the West, the cosmetics and gadgetry that we take for granted, but she always seemed too attached to her family to consider leaving. She must have seen my expression. 'Only for a visit, Auntie Sue. Just for a year perhaps.'

Next morning, I telephone the airport direct and ask if there are any flights to Heho. I am in luck. Whether this is the unique weekly plane I do not know, but there are indeed two seats on the clockwise run stopping first at Mandalay. The plane is at noon. For old times' sake, we visit the Dhammayangyi Temple. It has always been my favourite and this time I buy the Princess puppet to add to my collection.

Back at the hotel, as I am settling the bill, the Tourist Burma guide arrives unannounced and not in good humour. Why did I not keep my appointment with him at 9 in the lobby? He addresses the question exclusively to me, ignoring Aye-Aye-Moh. I inform him of our new plans. We are on our way to Heho and Taunggyi. His face darkens. There is no plane, he says. Just as there were no spare rooms in this hotel last night, I say boldly. We are still the only guests at the hotel.

'We are on our way to Heho, my niece and I,' I say, 'and then to Taunggyi.' For the first time he looks at Aye-Aye-Moh. In retrospect I suppose I was being reckless. It hadn't occurred to me that the law forbidding the Burmese to speak to foreign journalists would apply to members of one's own family. As for Aye-Aye-Moh, she did not seem troubled and returned the courier's basilisk stare with interest.

Our triumph was short-lived. It would be tempting to think that SLORC, in its omnipotence, could control even the weather. A severe storm was forecast and had just begun to blow in earnest when we landed in Mandalay. There was no question, said the pilot, of continuing on to Heho, the storm was coming from that direction. Depending on weather conditions, we would fly straight to Rangoon. In the meantime, he said, passengers could disembark and wait in the terminal for further information.

A guide in the familiar Tourist Burma uniform, white tailored shirt and bottle-green *longyi*, a woman this time, emerged from the crowd and made straight for Aye-Aye-Moh and myself. It wouldn't have been difficult to spot us, all the other passengers were businessmen, a mixture of Burmese and foreign, carrying briefcases.

'We have organised a city tour for you,' she said. She too ignored Aye-Aye-Moh. 'There is a bus outside with some French and German tourists on it. Please follow me. Here is a packed lunch,' and she produced the standard, dying cardboard box.

'What about my niece?' I said. 'We are travelling together.'

'The bus is only for tourists,' said the lady from Tourist Burma.

'I am sorry, in that case I won't come with you. I don't want a city tour anyway. I shall stay with my niece. If we need to go anywhere, I shall get us a taxi,' I said.

This was not a reply the guide was expecting. She looked momentarily baffled and then spoke rapidly to Aye-Aye-Moh in Burmese. Aye-Aye-Moh listened respectfully and then proceeded to give as good as she got.

'Wait here,' the guide said to me. 'I will telephone the office.' And she moved quickly away.

'What did she say to you?' I asked Aye-Aye-Moh. 'She sounded rather threatening.'

'It is all right, Auntie Sue. She said did I know I was not supposed to speak to foreigners and then I told her you are my auntie and then she said she would ask if I was allowed on the bus. I think she would prefer to have me on the bus rather than you and me wandering about on our own.'

Aye-Aye-Moh was right. When the guide returned, her face now wore a conciliatory expression. 'I have been authorised to take your niece on the city tour but we do not have a lunch-box for her,' was all she said. The French and German tourists who had been waiting patiently outside in the sweltering heat gave Aye-Aye-Moh curious glances but we were soon forgotten as the bus skirted Mandalay's famous landmarks. I was now quite at sea with my plans. I had hoped to get some good inside material from Auntie May and the family in Taunggyi, sufficiently removed, I thought, from Rangoon to allow me to operate safely. But if the plane was going straight to Rangoon, I was in a fix. Last time I made the journey from Mandalay to Taunggyi, it took ten hours and we had reserved bus tickets. The chances of Tourist Burma allowing me to escape from their clutches a second time seemed unlikely.

It was Aye-Aye-Moh who came up with a solution. If I could afford her plane ticket, she said, she would come to Rangoon with me and introduce me to friends who would talk to me. As long as I didn't identify them, it would be safe enough. She would give me the address of Toto's engineering college. 'Done,' I said.

Next day at first light, I took the ferry across the Rangoon river to Syriam to find Toto. Boat fares, unlike everything else, seem to have held their own in Burma. The forty-five-minute trip cost one *kyat* (10p). It couldn't have been much less when the Irrawaddy Flotilla Company reigned supreme before World War Two. We pass stately junks, with their dusty blue sails taut against the breeze, battered naval warships, dhows with pointed prows, fragile fishing boats.

Along with the valuable tracts of teak forest, the Government has sold fishing rights to Thailand, robbing hundreds of Burmese fishermen of their livelihood. Where the revenue from all this has gone is obvious. The Tatmadaw presence is everywhere. There must be five times as many soldiers in evidence than on my last visit. But the infrastructure of the country seems to be grinding to a halt. The lack of aeroplanes is just one example. When my Fokker Friendship landed in Rangoon the day before there were only two machines on the tarmac, an Otter and a chopper.

At Syriam I find a taxi to take me to the engineering college, half an hour's drive from the port.

'Have you come to see Mr Brown?' says the gateman suspiciously.

'Yes,' I say, wondering who Mr Brown could be. He turns out to be Herr Braun, principal of the college which was set up by the West Germans three years ago with nine German lecturers. Eight of them left in disgust in 1988 after the student demonstrations, only Herr Braun stayed on. Fortunately, neither he nor Toto can be located, since I'm having doubts about involving my nephew, especially after the gateman tells me what a great job the Tatmadaw is doing. I think I had better wait for Aye-Aye-Moh to find Toto for me, the security men are beginning to look suspicious.

A duty visit next. My husband's Uncle Archie, in South Harting, has asked me to visit his brother Fred's grave in the war cemetery at Htaukkyant, twenty-five miles north of the capital. 'Captain J. F. Russell MC, Royal Scots Attached Gurkha Rifles, 25 February 1945, aged thirty-two,' says the simple brass plaque, just one among 27,000 others. A huge yellow butterfly settles on the rose bush beside it.

Driving back, I spot a sign saying NLD District Office. The driver won't park directly outside, so I leave him in a tea-shop round the corner. In a small room with a couple of wooden tables, a quiet bespectacled man agrees to talk to me. As far as he is concerned, he says, I am not a foreigner (anyone can see that) so he is not breaking the law.

Yes, he knows people who have been arrested, disappeared or fled across the Thai border. What will happen if Suu Kyi is re-arrested? 'Nothing I hope,' says the quiet man. 'We will win but we must be patient. To protest would be madness. The army wants an excuse to clamp down.'

'How long will you wait?' I asked.

'As long as it takes,' he says.

Fired with eleventh-hour recklessness – I have only two more days in the country – I stop to take photographs of a slogan saying 'ONLY WITH DISCIPLINE CAN THERE BE PROGRESS'.

A figure in a blue *longyi* approaches. 'Are you a journalist?' he says.

'I am a tourist,' I say.

His name is Tommy, he was a medical student until Rangoon University closed. Could he have my malaria pills for his friends on the Thai border. He says the Government is offering the Thais 5000 *baht* (£125) for every Burmese repatriated. Four fellow-students were shot dead in front of him during the 1988 demonstrations. It is too dangerous to talk here, says Tommy. Behind us, a fortune-teller sitting under a tree with a client rolling dice looks up. Tommy asks him for some paper and writes down his address.

'I'll bring the pills tomorrow,' I promise.

At dawn, next morning, with Aye-Aye-Moh beside me in the taxi and the sound of a cock crowing noisily (how odd to hear a cock crowing in a capital city), we go to the address on the fortune-teller's scrap of paper. Tommy had said if there were any problems finding him, just ask for the house with the pianos. Tommy's district looks a bit like Molet Saung Gong, run-down and seedy, the buildings little more than shacks, but Tommy's does indeed have not one but two pianos in there among the usual assortment of furniture. Anyone's guess when either was last played. Their ivory keys, those that are left, are dark-brown with age. Tommy says his aunt used to play before she died.

What he tells me of the student demonstration and subsequent repression confirms everything that Amnesty put out at the time. The effect on Aye-Aye-Moh, however, is startling. Tommy has been speaking in tolerably good English, occasionally using my niece as an interpreter, but when he has finished his story they talk for a long time together in Burmese.

Back in the Strand, Aye-Aye-Moh tells me she has been thinking. She will tell me exactly what happened in Taunggyi when the army opened fire on the students but she will tell it into my tape-recorder in Burmese. She does not know enough English words to give the full story. When I get home, she says, I should give it to my mother to translate.

For a brief moment, family loyalties clash with professional interest. How dangerous is it for my niece to do this but then, on the other hand, just being with me for the last three days is breaking the law. Are you sure you want to? I say. If you think it might get you into trouble, I shall quite understand. We must not do it here in the hotel, there may be someone listening, is all she says. It is better to be outside in the park.

It has started to rain. Not the usual monsoon downpour but a fine, persistent drizzle. We walk to some gardens behind the Strand Hotel. In one corner there is a children's playground with slides, roundabouts and swings. Aye-Aye-Moh sits on one of the swings, it has a yellow seat. I pass her my dictaphone which she holds very close to her mouth like an ice-cream cornet. Then she starts speaking quite loudly into the microphone. Her delivery is sing-song like the *phongyi*'s chanting prayers and she keeps her eyes fixed on a point just beyond my shoulder. I feel rather stupid standing there and indicate that I will go for a stroll and come back in fifteen minutes. There is no one else in the park or on the streets, the rain is getting heavier.

There is something surreal about all this. Glancing over my shoulder I can see the tiny figure of my niece sitting bolt upright on the swing, talking into the tape, the rain dripping down her fringe into her eyes. If we were looking to do this discreetly we were going about it the wrong way. There could be few more suspicious sights than Aye-Aye-Moh talking to herself in the rain. We were sitting targets for SLORC attention.

My two remaining days in Burma have the same sense of unreality about them. Toto, my nephew, whose English is imperfect, was disinclined to tell me anything about his job, his employers or his views. I get a totally different picture of events from my Uncle Pe Kin whom I drop in to see the following afternoon. I have tried to telephone him first but his telephone is out of order. I have to ring long and hard on the bell beside the wrought-iron gates outside Uncle Pe Kin's residence before he finally appears. He is wearing a designer shirt and, unusual for him, a *longyi*, but that's because he wasn't expecting visitors. Normally he entertains in a linen Nehru-style jacket and immaculately creased slacks.

Unlike Toto, Uncle Pe Kin isn't at all reluctant to discuss the political situation. He positively relishes this opportunity to put me straight after all the nonsense written in the foreign press. Pouring large measures of single malt into crystal tumblers, he talks about the heroic stand taken by the military leaders in the terrible summer of 1988. 'Your Auntie Marjorie and I were in fear of our lives,' he says, inclining his head towards his wife.

Auntie Marjorie, tall for a Burmese, statuesque even, nods in agreement and returns to her task of smoothing down the lace armrests of her chair. She is still very house-proud I see.

'You cannot imagine how desperate the situation was with all those hooligans running riot,' continues Uncle Pe Kin. 'The reports say the Army opened fire on the demonstrators – believe me, it was precisely the reverse. It was the Communist infiltrators who attacked the soldiers. Take that occasion which the foreign press described as a massacre by the Army. The real story, and I got it from Saw Maung himself, was that the troops surrounded the demonstrators who were destroying everything in sight. They had their rifles ready but Saw Maung refused to give the order to shoot. "I want no bloodshed," he commanded. The mob grew more violent and the soldiers had to retreat to the first floor of the surrounding buildings. The officers begged Saw Maung to give the order to open fire but again he refused. "No bloodshed," he repeated. The soldiers retreated to the second floor and it was only when groups of militant *phongyis* actually disarmed some of the soldiers, stripped off their uniforms and forced them to wear monks' robes, that Saw Maung relented and ordered the troops to fire above the crowd. Well, he had to, didn't he? You cannot humiliate the Army and retain the respect of the people.'

Auntie Marjorie asks after my mother and my sister's family. 'You've just had a new baby, I hear. What's his name? Have you eaten yet, you must be tired . . .' She was ever a motherly soul.

Since my last visit, I have acquired another uncle. U Kyi Sein Gyi is a cousin of my mother's whom she had forgotten about until she went to a Bombay Burmah Trading Company Reunion Dinner the year before. Someone had mentioned a Burmese doctor in Liverpool, my mother knew the name, and the family tree in all its complexities was hauled out and examined in detail. The Burmese doctor's father was Uncle Kyi Sein Gyi.

Uncle Kyi Sein Gyi is a wheeler-dealer in the import/export line. When there are shortages of anything from light bulbs to lentils, somehow Uncle Kyi Sein Gyi could put his finger on them. This was useful the previous year when the country was in turmoil. Shortages were commonplace and Uncle Kyi did a roaring trade. Many of the Western embassy wives were sent to Bangkok for safety. It was not uncommon to see the diplomatic cars parked outside my uncle's house where he dispensed hospitality and a lavish spread to the remaining members of the diplomatic corps.

Uncle Kyi has something to celebrate. His son-in-law has just been elected an NLD member. The champagne is flowing and despite Aung San Suu Kyi's detention, the new MP is optimistic about his political future. 'There are too many people behind us to fail,' he said.

My last duty is at Molet Saung Gong. Auntie Betty is no longer here, Susan is now head of the family with her father, Uncle Sein Koh, a doddery figure who has to be taken care of. Susan is working as a primary schoolteacher, her older brother is still in prison, her younger ones seem to be heading that way, both caught up in Rangoon's burgeoning drug culture as well.

What does Uncle Sein Koh think about the election results? He is squatting on a small wooden stool, he has no teeth these days and his face looks sunken. He says he is too old to be interested in politics and that he understands the Army is doing a fine job.

Susan tells me she has been writing regularly to my mother since Auntie Betty died. She cannot leave Burma yet, she says, her father needs her, but her ambition is to come to England and maybe live with my mother, herself now a widow. She says she might also help me with my children, she knows of English families who have Burmese nannies.

I suspect she is forty years out of date. When the country

got its independence and the British went home for good, some of them took their Burmese *amahs* with them because they had become members of the family. There was one tragic story of a family who decided against taking the *amah*. I got this story from Auntie Patsy, she of the dark glasses and cigarette holder. Apparently the family explained they could not afford to keep a nanny in England and with much regret they would have to leave her behind. The *amah* begged to come with them, she said she didn't want payment, just a home. No, it would still not be possible. Weeping, she asked if she could come to the boat to see them off. There were three children, the smallest a child of six months. As the boat was about to depart and visitors were ordered to disembark, the *amah*, holding the baby, pleaded one last time for the family to change their mind and take her. Alas, no, they said. Whereupon the demented woman threw herself overboard with the baby. They were both drowned.

The complexities of getting Susan a visa and ticket to come to England are daunting. Five years on, we are still filling in forms and trying to make sense of the documentation necessary for her to spend six months with us. Ominously, all communication with her has now ceased. Uncle Sein Koh died two years ago and there is nothing, she says, to keep her in Burma. My long-term plan would be for her to come and act as a companion to my mother and, with any luck, find herself a British husband to enable her to stay on. My mother has the spare room ready.

The first time I wrote about my Burmese connections in the *Observer*, I received a mixed bag of letters. Some were from servicemen who remembered their time in Burma with nostalgia, others were from Women's Institutes asking me to come and talk to their members about my fascinating roots. The ones I chiefly remember, and there were half a dozen or so of these, were from Anglo-Burmese ladies my mother's age who congratulated me on having the courage (their word) to admit that I was Burmese. One woman writing from the Midlands said she had always tried to keep her Anglo-Burmese origins a secret. She made it sound like a criminal record but then for thirty-odd years I had felt pretty much the same way.

When I started writing this book I said that all I ever wanted was to be English. I am not sure what that means any more. I have just been to collect my five-year-old son from a typical inner London State Primary school and watching the children come out I am struck by the multitude of races represented. This doesn't apply just to that age group, both my older daughters, now at university, have very few friends who would fit into my mother's definition of 'English'. I no longer feel the odd one out and it may be my imagination but fewer people ask me where I am from *originally*. Maybe it is because I feel more relaxed about myself, having been to Burma and discovered my other half. There are aspects of the Burmese character that I should dearly love to have myself, their serenity, their grace, their gentleness. I would especially like my children, typical street-wise London kids, to inherit some of those aspects too. On the other hand I realise, with a tinge of sadness, that I could never join my female cousins pounding *balachan* in the kitchen while their husbands talked to foreign visitors in the front room. When, if, my niece Susan arrives to live with us, she too, I suspect, will gradually forget that serenity, that passivity synonymous with Burmese women. Or am I being ridiculously idealistic? The turbulent events in Burma over the last five years have probably put paid to that already.

When Barbra Streisand first became famous, an interviewer asked where she was born. She didn't want to say Brooklyn, so she named the most exotic-sounding place she could think of. 'Rangoon,' she replied. In the old days when people asked me where I was from I would have given anything to say Bournemouth. Miss Streisand wanted to be exotic, I just wanted to be ordinary. Now I am only too happy to talk at length about the Burmese connection.

An economist friend came over the other day and was talking about the new growth areas of the world. Burma was at the top of the list. 'You mark my words,' he said. 'Burma will have the same booming economy as South Korea and as many tourists as Thailand.' It sounds as though I got there just in time.

Glossary

arnadeh   politeness
amah   nanny
balachan   pickle
brinjal   a Burmese vegetable
Daw   Mrs
derzi   tailor (Ind)
gille dundoo   a stick-and-ball game
guang phyn thakin gyi   big white boss
ka bia   half and half
kador, kador   forgive me
kauk-sweh   noodle and vegetable dish
Ko Ko   big brother
kway Kalas   dog-Indian
kyat   unit of currency
lepet   a delicacy made from shredded ginger and green tea
longyi   wrap-round garment tucked in at waist worn by
  both sexes
Ma   Miss
Ma Ma Gyi   big sister
Ma Ma Lay   little sister

maidan   parade-ground (Ind)
mali   gardener (Ind)
maung   boy
nun deh   give me a kiss (literally a sniff)
nyat   guardian spirit
nyi   red, little
Nyi Nyi   little brother
oozie   elephant minder
phongyi   Buddhist monk
pwe   a Burmese dance
pya   unit of currency (100 pya = 1 kyat)
shi-ko   Burmese obeisance
shin-pyu   the ceremony of taking monks' vows
SLORC   State Law and Order Restoration Council
stik lak   lacquer
syce   groom (Ind)
Tatmadaw   Burmese Army
thakin   master
thakin ma gyi   the big mistress
thanaka   Burmese cosmetics
U   Mr